£1 Thursdays

Kat Rose-Martin

T0188679

methuen | drama

LONDON • NEW YORK • OXFORD • NEW DELHI • SYDNEY

METHUEN DRAMA
Bloomsbury Publishing Plc
50 Bedford Square, London, WC1B 3DP, UK
1385 Broadway, New York, NY 10018, USA
29 Earlsfort Terrace, Dublin 2, Ireland

BLOOMSBURY, METHUEN DRAMA and the Methuen
Drama logo are trademarks of Bloomsbury Publishing Plc

First published in Great Britain 2023

Copyright © Kat Rose-Martin, 2023

Kat Rose-Martin has asserted her right under the Copyright, Designs
and Patents Act, 1988, to be identified as author of this work.

Cover image © Shutterstock

All rights reserved. No part of this publication may be reproduced or
transmitted in any form or by any means, electronic or mechanical, including
photocopying, recording, or any information storage or retrieval system,
without prior permission in writing from the publishers.

Bloomsbury Publishing Plc does not have any control over, or responsibility
for, any third-party websites referred to or in this book. All internet addresses
given in this book were correct at the time of going to press. The author and
publisher regret any inconvenience caused if addresses have changed or sites
have ceased to exist, but can accept no responsibility for any such changes.

No rights in incidental music or songs contained in the work are hereby
granted and performance rights for any performance/presentation
whatsoever must be obtained from the respective copyright owners.

All rights whatsoever in this play are strictly reserved and application
for performance etc. should be made before rehearsals to United Agents,
12–26 Lexington Street, London, W1F 0LE. No performance
may be given unless a licence has been obtained.

A catalogue record for this book is available from the British Library.

A catalog record for this book is available from the Library of Congress.

ISBN: PB: 978-1-3504-5636-5
ePDF: 978-1-3504-5637-2
eBook: 978-1-3504-5638-9

Series: Modern Plays

Typeset by Mark Heslington Ltd, Scarborough, North Yorkshire

To find out more about our authors and books visit
www.bloomsbury.com and sign up for our newsletters.

Julia Blomberg for £1 Thursdays Ltd
in association with
Neil McPherson for the Finborough Theatre
presents

The world premiere

£1 Thursdays

by Kat Rose-Martin

First performance at the Finborough Theatre:
Tuesday, 28 November 2023.

Supported using public funding by the National Lottery through Arts Council England

Supported using public funding by
**ARTS COUNCIL
ENGLAND**

£1 Thursdays

by Kat Rose-Martin

Cast in order of appearance

Jen	**Yasmin Taheri**
Stacey	**Monique Ashe-Palmer**
Leanne	**Sian Breckin**
Nurse	**Sian Breckin**
Nathan	**Joseph Ayre**
Tristan	**Joseph Ayre**

The action takes place in Bradford, 2012.

The approximate running time is 90 minutes.

There will be no interval.

Director	**Vicky Moran**
Set and Costume Designer	**Ethan Cheek**
Lighting Designer	**Rajiv Pattani**
Sound Designer	**Roly Botha**
Movement Director	**Nadia Sohawon**
Intimacy Director	**Raniah Al-Sayed**
Fight Director	**Sam Behan**
Wellbeing Support	**Stacey Permaul**
Stage Manager	**Reuben Bojang**
Producer	**Julia Blomberg**

Face masks are optional, except on Covid Safe Sunday matinees when they are mandatory.

Please turn your mobile phones off – the light they emit can be distracting.

Our patrons are respectfully reminded that, in this intimate theatre, any noise such as the rustling of programmes, talking or the ringing of mobile phones may distract the actors and your fellow audience members.

We regret there is no admittance or re-admittance to the auditorium whilst the performance is in progress.

Monique Ashe-Palmer | Stacey

Trained at Bird College.

Theatre includes *Six* (Vaudeville Theatre), *Waitress* (Adelphi Theatre and national tour), *Madagascar the Musical* (national and international tour) and *Sleeping Beauty* (Camberley Theatre).

Associate choreography includes *Madagascar the Musical* (national and international tour).

Television includes *Emmerdale*.

Joseph Ayre | Nathan and Tristan

Trained at East 15 Acting School.

Theatre includes *The Curious Incident of the Dog in the Night-Time* (National Theatre and Gielgud Theatre) and *The Cask of Amontillado* (Old Red Lion Theatre).

Television includes *Doctors* and *Flatmates*.

Radio includes *Operation Crucible*, *Borstal Boy*, *Life Lines* and *Keeping the Wolf Out*.

Sian Breckin | Leanne and Nurse

Theatre includes *Primetime* (Royal Court Theatre), *Yen* (Royal Court Theatre and Royal Exchange Theatre, Manchester), *Geisha Girls* and *Chalet Lines* (Bush Theatre), *But I Cd Only Whisper* (Arcola Theatre) and *Old Vic New Voices – Twenty-Four Hour Plays* (The Old Vic).

Film includes *V.S*, *Starred Up*, *Tyrannosaur* and *Donkey Punch*.

Television includes *The Bay II*, *Language of Love/ Sommaren-85*, *Kiri*, *The Trial*, *The Watchman*, *Houdini and Doyle*, *Silent Witness*, *Truckers*, *Dates*, *Casualty*, *Scott and Bailey*, *D.C.I. Banks: Aftermath*, *Heartbeat*, *George Gently*, *The Bill* and *The Royal*.

Yasmin Taheri | Jen

Trained at the Royal Academy of Dramatic Art.

Theatre includes *Henry VI Parts II and III*, *The Merchant of Venice*, *Tartuffe* and *Tamburlaine* (Royal Shakespeare Company).

Television includes *Open Wide*, *Holby City*, *Ladhood*, *Murder in Provence* and *The Long Shadow*.

Kat Rose-Martin | Playwright

Kat is a Bradford-born and based writer and actor, and the inaugural winner of the Kay Mellor Fellowship. She was recently nominated for the Royal Television Society Yorkshire One to Watch Award. In 2020, she was part of BBC Writers Room Northern Voices. In 2021, she was selected for Sky Comedy Rep – a writers' scheme with Birmingham Rep and Sky TV.

Theatre includes *Aphra Behn* (Shakespeare's Globe), *Jane Hair* (Brontë Society), *Shit but Mine* (Paines Plough), *Children of War* (Sheffield Theatres), *Whooosh* (Pilot Theatre), *Pick N Mix* (Leeds Studio and Pleasance), the development of *£1 Thursdays* (Stockroom, formerly Out of Joint), *End Cubicle* (High Tide and Sheffield Theatres) and *Cheap as Chips* (Leeds Playhouse).

Television includes the 2021 Christmas episode of *Holby City*, an ADHD diagnosis story in *The Dumping Ground* (CBBC), two episodes of *Waterloo Road* (BBC, Wall to Wall and Rope Ladder), and the forthcoming *Beyond Paradise* (BBC1) and *Dinosaur* (BBC Comedy). Her television drama *The Crossleys* made the BAFTA Rocliffe TV Drama Top 10 and is now in development in the US. She has original television projects in development with Rollem, Abbotvision, Warp, Wall to Wall and BBC Scotland, Urban Myths, Red Planet and Avalon. She has had pilot commissions with BBC3 and BBC Comedy. Her script *Ursula,* developed with RED Productions, made The Brit List 2021. She has also been part of the LA Writers Room for *Day 1's* (Matthew Vaughn, Doug Ellin and Hera Pictures). She was also in the Writers Rooms for series two of Paul Abbott's *Wolfe* (Sky Max), and co-writing an episode of Alex De Rakoff's '*X*' (Gaumont US). In 2023, she also acted as a consultant for *Hollyoaks*.

Vicky Moran | Director

Theatre includes *In the Net* (Jermyn Street Theatre), *No Sweat* (Pleasance London), *Nomad* (Tramshed), *Khojaly* (Union Theatre) and *Life in the UK* (Theatre503).

Assistant direction includes *Cathy* (national tour).

Vicky is a theatre director working predominantly in new writing. She is the Director of women-led company *In Her Strength,* who have created work for Camden People's Theatre, Arts Depot, and The Y Theatre, Leicester. Vicky was the Associate Director at Cardboard Citizens as part of WJCB Bursary Award in 2017–19. She was the Artist in Residence at Arts Depot for 2023, as well as Visiting Project Associate at the Young Vic 2022/23. Vicky has also delivered extensive creative projects for Donmar Warehouse, National Theatre, Clean Break, Kiln Theatre and the Old Vic.

Ethan Cheek | Set and Costume Designer

Trained at the Royal Central School of Speech and Drama.

Theatre includes *Shock Horror* (national tour), *Into the Woods* and *The Baker's Wife* (Playground Theatre), *Borders* (Vaults), *The Scar Test*, *Little Sweet Thing* and *Blister* (London Academy of Music and Dramatic Art), *The Concrete Jungle Book* (Pleasance London), *Rabbit Hole* for which he was nominated for an OffWestEnd Award for Best Set Design (Union Theatre), *The Bridges of Madison County* (Quick Fantastic) and *Spring Awakening* (Royal Central School of Speech and Drama).

Associate and assistant design credits include work with Rosanna Vize, Justin Williams, Ryan Dawson Laight, Andrew Exeter, Alex Berry, Lee Newby and David Woodhead.

Rajiv Pattani | Lighting Designer

Trained at the London Academy of Music and Dramatic Art.

Theatre includes *High Times and Dirty Monsters* (national tour), *Strategic Love Play* (Soho Theatre and Paines Plough tour), *The Garden of Words* (Park Theatre), *Zoe's Peculiar Journey Through Time* (Southbank Centre and national tour), *Hairy* (Polka Theatre), *The Flood* (Queen's Theatre, Hornchurch), *Smoke* and *Yellowfin* (Southwark Playhouse), *Alice in Wonderland* (Poltergeist Theatre Company and Brixton House), *Yellowman*, *Statements After an Arrest Under the Immorality Act* and *Outside* (Orange Tree Theatre), *Hungry* (Soho Theatre, Paines Plough and Roundabout),

Supernova (Theatre503 and national tour), *Wolfie* (Theatre503), *The White Card* (Northern Stage, Leeds Playhouse, Birmingham Rep, Soho Theatre and HOME Manchester), *Mog the Forgetful Cat* (Royal and Derngate Theatres, Northampton, and national tour), *Kabul Goes Pop! Television Music Afghanistan!* (Brixton House and national tour), *Pilgrims* (Guildhall School of Music and Drama), *Sorry, You're Not a Winner* (Paines Plough tour), *Winners* (Theatre on the Downs and Wardrobe Ensemble), *Final Farewell, Dawaat* (Tara Theatre), *Hunger* (Arcola Theatre), *Dirty Crusty* (Yard Theatre), *Dismantle This Room* (Jerwood Theatre Downstairs), *Nassim* (Bush Theatre, Traverse Theatre, Edinburgh, and international tour) and *Babylon Beyond Boarders, Leave Taking* and *Ramona Tells Jim* (Bush Theatre).

Roly Botha | Sound Designer

Theatre includes *Shut Up, I'm Dreaming* (National Theatre), *Truth and Tails* (Chichester Festival Theatre), *Tambo and Bones* (Theatre Royal Stratford East), *The Ultimate Pickle, A Sudden Violent Burst of Rain* and *Half Empty Glasses* (Paines Plough), *Orlando* (Jermyn Street Theatre), *Boys* (Barbican, Southbank Centre and national tour), *Coming to England* (Birmingham Repertory Theatre), *Wild* (Unicorn Theatre), *Muck* and *Warheads* (Park Theatre), *Blowhole* (Soho Theatre), *Milk and Gall* (Theatre503), *Fritz and Matlock* (Pleasance Theatre), *Helen* (Battersea Arts Centre), *Brother* (Southwark Playhouse), *Girls, Care* (national tour for The PappyShow) and *Making Fatiha* (Camden People's Theatre).

Roly (they/them) is a composer, sound designer and an Associate Artist of The PappyShow.

Reuben Bojang | Stage Manager

Theatre includes *Pals* and *Romeo and Juliet* (Tabard Theatre), *Henry V – Lion of England, Hamlet – Horatio's Tale* and *The Marilyn Conspiracy* (Edinburgh Fringe), *Walking to Jerusalem* (regional tour), *Under Milk Wood* (Filodrammatici Theatre, Milan and regional tour), *A Christmas Carol* (Teatro Litta, Milan, regional tour and Edinburgh Fringe), *Snatched!* (White Bear Theatre), *9 Circles* (Park Theatre and Edinburgh Fringe), Make Mine a Double Season (Park Theatre), *Pickle* (Park Theatre, The Radlett Centre and Soho Theatre), *Picasso* (Playground Theatre and Edinburgh Fringe), *Right Dishonourable Friend* (VAULT Festival), *Animal* (Park Theatre, Hope Mill Theatre, Manchester and Bristol Tobacco Factory) and *Tomorrow Is Already Dead* (Soho Theatre and Latitude Festival).

Julia Blomberg | Producer

Previous productions at the Finborough Theatre include associate producer for *The Wind and the Rain* and *The Retreat*.

Trained in Arts Policy and Management at Birkbeck, University of London.

Theatre includes *Robot Penguin* (Wanstead Fringe), *The Language of Angels*, *Much Ado About Nothing* and *The Importance of Being Earnest* (Rooke Theater, South Hadley, Massachusetts).

Production Acknowledgements

Social Media Marketing | **Lâl Yolgeçenli**

Press Photography | **Ali Wright**

Production Photography | **Alex Brenner**

Press Representative | **Storytelling PR**

Charity Partner | **Advance Charity**

Special thanks to:

Stockroom Productions, Hawkseed Theatre, Avalon, Jennifer Thomas.

FINBOROUGH THEATRE

"**Probably the most influential fringe theatre in the world.**" *Time Out*

"**Not just a theatre, but a miracle.**" *Metro*

"**The mighty little Finborough which, under Neil McPherson, continues to offer a mixture of neglected classics and new writing in a cannily curated mix.**" Lyn Gardner, *The Stage*

"**The tiny but mighty Finborough.**" Ben Brantley, *The New York Times*

Founded in 1980, the multi-award-winning Finborough Theatre presents plays and music theatre, concentrated exclusively on vibrant new writing and unique rediscoveries from the 19th and 20th centuries, both in our 154-year-old home and online through our #FinboroughFrontier digital initiative.

Our programme is unique – we never present work that has been seen anywhere in London during the last 25 years. Behind the scenes, we continue to discover and develop a new generation of theatre makers. Despite remaining completely unsubsidised, the Finborough Theatre has an unparalleled track record for attracting the finest talent who go on to become leading voices in British theatre. Under Artistic Director Neil McPherson, it has discovered some of the UK's most exciting new playwrights including Laura Wade, James Graham, Mike Bartlett, Jack Thorne, Carmen Nasr, Athena Stevens and Anders Lustgarten, and directors including Tamara Harvey, Robert Hastie, Tom Littler, Blanche McIntyre, Kate Wasserberg and Sam Yates.

Artists working at the theatre in the 1980s included Clive Barker, Rory Bremner, Nica Burns, Kathy Burke, Ken Campbell, Jane Horrocks, Nicola Walker and Claire Dowie. In the 1990s, the Finborough Theatre first became known for new writing including Naomi Wallace's first play *The War Boys*, Rachel Weisz in David Farr's *Neville Southall's Washbag*, four plays by Anthony Neilson including *Penetrator* and *The Censor*, both of which transferred to the Royal Court Theatre, and new plays by Richard Bean, Lucinda Coxon, David Eldridge and Tony Marchant. New writing development included the premieres of modern classics such as Mark Ravenhill's *Shopping and F**king*, Conor McPherson's *This Lime Tree Bower*, Naomi Wallace's *Slaughter City* and Martin McDonagh's *The Pillowman*.

Since 2000, new British plays have included Laura Wade's London debut *Young Emma* (commissioned by the Finborough Theatre), James Graham's London debut *Albert's Boy* with Victor Spinetti and four other of his first plays, Sarah Grochala's *S27*, Athena Stevens' *Schism* which was nominated for an Olivier Award, and West End transfers for Joy Wilkinson's *Fair*, Nicholas de Jongh's *Plague Over England*, Jack Thorne's *Fanny and Faggot*, Neil McPherson's Olivier Award nominated *It Is Easy to Be Dead* and Dawn King's *Foxfinder*.

UK premieres of foreign plays have included plays by Lanford Wilson, Larry Kramer, Tennessee Williams and Suzan-Lori Parks, the English premieres of two Scots language classics by Robert McLellan and more Canadian plays than any other theatre in Europe, with West End transfers for Frank McGuinness' *Gates of Gold* with William Gaunt and Craig Higginson's *Dream of the Dog* with Dame Janet Suzman. In December 2022, the Finborough Theatre became the first foreign theatre to perform in Ukraine since the Russian invasion with *Pussycat in Memory of Darkness* which has subsequently revisited Kyiv, and played in Germany and the USA.

Rediscoveries of neglected work – most commissioned by the Finborough Theatre – have included the first London revivals of Rolf Hochhuth's *Soldiers* and *The Representative*, both parts of Keith Dewhurst's *Lark Rise to Candleford*, *Etta Jenks* with Clarke Peters and Daniela Nardini, three rediscoveries from Noël Coward and Lennox Robinson's *Drama at Inish* with Celia Imrie and Paul O'Grady. Transfers have included Emlyn Williams' *Accolade* and John Van Druten's *London Wall* to St James' Theatre, and J. B. Priestley's *Cornelius* to a sell-out Off Broadway run in New York City.

Music theatre has included the new (premieres from Craig Adams, Grant Olding, Charles Miller, Michael John LaChuisa, Adam Guettel, Andrew Lippa, Paul Scott Goodman, Polly Pen and Adam Gwon's *Ordinary Days* which transferred to the West End) and the old (the UK premiere of Rodgers and Hammerstein's *State Fair* which also transferred to the West End), and the acclaimed 'Celebrating British Music Theatre' series.

The Finborough Theatre won the 2020 and 2022 London Pub Theatres Pub Theatre of the Year Award, *The Stage* Fringe Theatre of the Year Award in 2011, the Empty Space Peter Brook Award in 2010 and 2012, and was nominated for an Olivier Award in 2017 and 2019. Artistic Director Neil McPherson was awarded the Critics' Circle Special Award for Services to Theatre in 2019. It is the only unsubsidised theatre ever to be awarded the Channel 4 Playwrights Scheme bursary twelve times.

www.finboroughtheatre.co.uk

FINBOROUGH THEATRE

118 Finborough Road, London SW10 9ED
admin@finboroughtheatre.co.uk
www.finboroughtheatre.co.uk

Artistic Director | **Neil McPherson**
Founding Director | **Phil Willmott**
Resident Designer | **Alex Marker**
General Managers | **Ellie Renfrew** and **Caitlin Carr**
Assistant General Managers | **Maddy D-Houston** and **Dylan Harvey**
Fundraising Director | **Jonathan Ellicott**
Playwrights in Residence | **James Graham, Dawn King, Anders Lustgarten, Carmen Nasr, Athena Stevens**
Playwright on Attachment | **Saana Sze**
Peggy Ramsay Foundation / Film 4 Awards Scheme Playwright (Tom Erhardt Bursary) | **Sophie Swithinbank**
Technical Manager | **Angus Chisholm**
Literary Manager | **Sue Healy**
Deputy Literary Manager | **Rhys Hayes**
Literary Assistants | **Sibylla Kalid, Beth Duke, Ella Fidler** and **Ella Gold**
Literary Assistant (International) | **Sarah Jane Schostack** and **Rebecca Hagberg Snäckerström**
Associate Producer | **Arsalan Sattari**
Associate Sound Designer | **Julian Starr**
Book Keeper | **Patti Williams**
Board of Trustees | **Michele Gorgodian, Robbie Kings, Russell Levinson, Pembe Al Mazrouei, John Terry** and **Anna-Marie Wallis**
And our volunteers.

The Finborough Theatre is a member of the Independent Theatre Council, the Society of Independent Theatres, Musical Theatre Network, The Friends of Brompton Cemetery, The Earl's Court Society, The Kensington Society, and the WEST Theatre Association, Kyiv, Ukraine.

Supported by

The Finborough Theatre has the support of the Peggy Ramsay Foundation / Film 4 Playwrights Awards Scheme.

Mailing
Email admin@finboroughtheatre.co.uk or give your details to our Box Office staff to join our free email list.

Playscripts
Many of the Finborough Theatre's plays have been published and are on sale from our website.

Environment
The Finborough Theatre has a 100% sustainable electricity supply.

Local History
The Finborough Theatre's local history website is online at **www.earlscourtlocalhistory.co.uk**

The Finborough Theatre on Social Media

 www.facebook.com/FinboroughTheatre

 www.twitter.com/finborough

 www.instagram.com/finboroughtheatre

 www.youtube.com/@finboroughtheatre

 www.tiktok.com/@finboroughtheatre

 www.threads.net/@finboroughtheatre

Friends of the Finborough Theatre
The Finborough Theatre is a registered charity. We receive no public funding, and rely solely on the support of our audiences.

Please do consider supporting us by joining our **newly relaunched** Friends of the Finborough Theatre scheme.

There are five categories of Friends, each offering a wide range of benefits.

Please ask any member of our staff for a leaflet.

William Terriss Friends – Anonymous. Patrick Foster. Janet and Leo Liebster. Ros and Alan Haigh.

Adelaide Neilson Friends – Charles Glanville. Philip G Hooker.

Legacy Gifts – Tom Erhardt.

Smoking is not permitted in the auditorium.
The videotaping or making of electronic or other audio and/or visual recordings or streams of this production is strictly prohibited.

In accordance with the requirements of the Royal Borough of Kensington and Chelsea:
1. The public may leave at the end of the performance by all doors and such doors must at that time be kept open.
2. All gangways, corridors, staircases and external passageways intended for exit shall be left entirely free from obstruction whether permanent or temporary.
3. Persons shall not be permitted to stand or sit in any of the gangways intercepting the seating or to sit in any of the other gangways.

The Finborough Theatre is a registered charity and a company limited by guarantee. Registered in England and Wales no. 03448268. Registered Charity no. 1071304. Registered Office: 118 Finborough Road, London SW10 9ED.

£1 Thursdays

Characters

Jen Mason, *seventeen years old, from Bradford. Stacey's best friend.*
Stacey Blackwell, *seventeen years old, from Bradford. Jen's best friend.*
Leanne Mason, *fifty years old, from Bradford. Jen's mum.*
Nathan, *twenty-six years old, from Bradford. Stacey's boyfriend.*
Nurse, *fifty-two years old, from Bradford.*
Tristan, *twenty-seven years old, from Bradford but lost his accent. PhD student.*

Note

None of the characters should be presented as 'rough'. They are working class. They graft and they have it hard but they take pride in who they are. Swearing is a part of their everyday language and should be treated as such.

The play is set in Bradford in 2012.

It revolves around Club Ocean, a nightclub that plays chart music as well as classics from the past, such as 'Mr Brightside', 'SexyBack', Eminem and Spice Girls.

Glossary for non-Bradford speakers

Treat (pronounced tret) – Yorkshire for treated.

Doilum (pronounced doy-lum) – A fool.

Chatha's (pronounced chat-erz) – A corner shop.

Slam (pronounced slam) – To skive when referring to school or lessons.

Act One

Scene One: Forearms

A Thursday in mid-December. 3 a.m. Two lasses, aged seventeen, but look older, are stood outside Club Ocean near a taxi rank. They are wearing short skirts/shorts and low-cut tops. They look physically quite different. 'Single Ladies' by Beyoncé (or similar) plays out in the background.

Jen   You like him.

Stacey   Fuck off!

Jen   You do! I know you do.

Stacey   Don't.

Jen   You've got that look in yer eye.

Stacey   What look?

Jen   That half-squint, half-stoned look.

Stacey   You chat shit you do.

Jen   Don't.

Stacey   Besides he's far too mature for me. Got a job, drives a van, only drinks at weekends.

Jen   What's he doing out on a Thursday then?

Stacey   Boss isn't in tomorrow, means he can start late.

Jen   Right. Did ya pull him then or just chat about his schedule?

Stacey   Pulled him, but it were a bit, you know –

Jen   What?

Stacey   Wet.

Jen   You got –

Stacey   No, you fanny, his mouth wa, you know –

Jen   Hate to break it to you love, but mouths usually are.

Stacey   Anyway, I'm just not sure what I make of him yet.

Jen   I think you should give him a chance. He has nice . . . forearms.

Stacey   Forearms?

Jen   Yeh. Like just the right amount of hair, you know. Manly but not gorilla-y like.

Stacey   I'm hardly gonna jump in bed with him because he's got nice forearms, Jen.

Jen   I would.

Stacey   Yeh, well, we all know that.

Jen   Oi!

Stacey   Talking about jumping in bed, did I see you chatting to Stefan?

Jen   For a grand total of ten seconds.

Stacey   He's fit though in't he?

Jen   So fit.

Stacey   So fucking fit. I'm not sure about the neck tattoo though. What's that all about? Did you ask him?

Jen   I barely said 'Y'alright?' let alone, 'Why you've got "Ar Kid" tattooed on your neck?' Jeez, Stace, give us a chance.

Stacey   Still –

Jen   You going in tomorrow?

Stacey   I've got General Studies third period then Sports last. Might come in for 11. You've got Psychology fourth period on a Friday haven't you? You coming in for it?

Jen   I don't know, I fell out with Mr Jackson last week didn't I, so not feeling it.

Stacey   You've gotta make up with him though, Jen, or he'll give you a shit mark in your coursework.

Jen   He's gonna give me a shit mark anyway, probs cos I won't suck him off. He was bang out of order kicking me out of class. My shorts weren't even that short. Besides, if they were meant to be long, they'd be called longs wouldn't they, or culottes, but not fucking shorts. And I don't get why I get booted out, because what – my legs might distract fucking Zane in the corner. Kid could do with looking at a pair of real legs instead of them on Japanese cartoons.

Stacey   It's probably because you kicked off that he booted you out.

Jen   And it's my fucking right to kick off, I don't get what my legs have to do with my education anyway. And I'm not just going to sit there and take it when he gives me a warning for wearing fucking shorts. The guy's off his head and the system's fucked.

Stacey   If it's any constellation, I think you've got gorgeous legs, he's probably jealous.

Jen   'Constellation'? It's 'consolation', you doilum!

Stacey   Doilum? What are we, eight?

Jen   Stefan said he's coming out on Saturday as well, can get us in for cheap before 9 p.m.

Stacey   Teaching Sunday aren't I? Under-tens street dance. Prepping for the Christmas show. They're really coming on.

Jen   But Stefan?

Stacey   What's your plan for him? Make him your number forty-four?

Jen He's more of a graft than that. Might have to be number fifty-six or something? That's why we need to go on Saturday.

Stacey I've got to get up at 8 a.m.

Jen So go to bed at 3. Five hours is enough for anyone. You don't even want to be a teacher, it should be you dancing not the ten-year-olds.

Stacey It's money until I can afford to do classes or even train.

Jen There's no better training than the Ocean dancefloor.

Stacey I'll think about it.

Jen Right, I'm going to get in that taxi.

Stacey Alright. Giz a kiss. Please come in tomorrow, Jen, even if it's just so I don't have to sit with the knob squad for dinner.

Jen I'll message you when I get up, let you know if I'm hanging.

Stacey Please . . .

Jen Ta-ra. Text us when you're home safe.

Stacey Always.

Jen Love ya.

> **Jen** *exits.* **Stacey** *exits in opposite direction.*

Scene Two: STI Results

> *The Tuesday after.* **Jen** *and* **Stacey** *are dancing in* **Jen**'s *room. They are wearing T-shirts and knickers that say 'Sexy Chick, Sexy Check'. They sing along to 'Sexy Bitch' by Akon and David Guetta. They replace 'sexy bitch' with 'sexy check'.*

Stacey   This is my new move for Thursday. Swish your hair, dip the hip, flirty look and flutter, then turn as if you're not interested. What d'ya reck?

Jen   That's fit, that is.

Stacey   It's like a honey trap, I reckon.

Jen   Teach us then.

> **Stacey** *demonstrates for* **Jen**. **Stacey** *is a tad more coy with her moves, whereas as* **Jen** *goes for the full-on approach.*

Stacey   So, it's . . . swish hair, dip hip, flirty flutter, and turn away.

> **Jen** *copies.*

Jen   Swish hair.

Stacey   Dip hip. Flirty flutter.

> **Jen** *tries to flutter but she just blinks excessively.*

Jen   And turn away.

Stacey   That's it.

Jen   Think I'm gonna lose the flutter. Look like I'm having a fit. I'll add a pout instead.

Stacey   Right, so. Swish. Dip. Pout and turn.

Jen   Swish. Dip. Pout and turn.

> **Jen** *gets better and they do it in unison.*

Stacey   Ready? Go.

> *They stand facing outwards and do the move as if on a catwalk.*

Stacey   Nailed it.

Jen   I think it needs a slut drop at the end.

Stacey   Really?

Jen   It's good, don't get me wrong, but check this.

Jen *demonstrates. She is fierce. The slut drop is sexy as hell and she takes her time over it.*

Jen   Swish. Dip. Pout and turn then slut drop! Show 'em what they're missing.

They each practise a slut drop and playfully get out of hand then fall about in laughter.

Stacey's *phone goes off.*

Jen   He's a bit keen isn't he?

Stacey   Says he wants to take me out next week.

Jen   Where?

Stacey   Don't know.

Jen   Well, make sure it's not somewhere skanky.

Stacey   Yeh . . . You sure I should go? He's just a bit –

Jen   Listen, he seems nice enough, just give it a go, nothing to lose.

Stacey   Yeh, you're right. And his eyes are proper dreamy like.

Stacey *is excited to see him and have* **Jen**'s *approval.* **Stacey**'s *phone goes off again.*

Jen   Bloody hell, double text. Bit desperate.

Stacey *reads the message.*

Stacey   'Results negative'. Eh?

Jen   That must be from the test.

Stacey   Negative though? What's that? Does that mean it's a bad result or that they couldn't find owt there.

Jen   It means your clear, babe. No clap in your trap!

They laugh. **Jen**'s *phone goes off, she checks it.*

Jen   Fuck.

A pause. **Jen** *passes her phone to* **Stacey**.

Stacey (*reads*)   Results available . . . Shit, mate.

Leanne, **Jen**'s *mum, knocks on the bedroom door and comes straight in.*

Jen   MUM!

Leanne   What's going on in here?

Jen   You could've knocked!

Leanne   I did.

Jen   Yeh, but –

Stacey   I don't mind! Come on in, Leanne. How's your day been?

Leanne   Mad busy, thanks for asking, pet. Saw your mam today at the med centre, with one of the twins.

Stacey   Which one?

Leanne   Something about an ear infection?

Stacey   That'll be our Milo. The little shit's been desperate for attention, I swear he makes it up.

Leanne   Your poor mam looked knackered.

Stacey   I'm not surprised, she doesn't get a second for herself. She's been on the nights and with me dad working away at the moment, she's got the whole crowd to look after and our Aidy hardly helps out as much as he could. I'm glad to get a breather to be honest.

Leanne   You're giving her a hand though?

Stacey   Course. I look after our Jay loads but there's only so many nappies I can change when it weren't even me who chose to pop out another kid. Still, it wouldn't shock me if they had a sixth, pretty sure at this rate, she could sneeze and a kid would appear from the darkness.

She gestures Mystic Meg style from her downstairs.

Jen   Ew.

Leanne   Oi! We practically tear ourselves in two for you, so you don't get to comment about our nethers thanks very much.

Jen   Fair.

Stacey   Hey, Leanne, check out our matching knicks!

Jen   Stace!

Stacey   We got 'em free at school for taking an STI check.

Stacey *stands up and shows the back of her underwear to* **Leanne**.

Stacey   Sexy Chick. Sexy Check! Geddit?

Leanne   No?

Stacey   Chick. Check! Cos we had an STI check. Piss in a cup, get a free pair of knicks!

Leanne   Oh that's good! Oh I love them! Very trendy aren't they? You should've got me a pair! I could pull those off. I'll piss in a cup and send it in with you tomorrow.

Jen   Muuum!

Leanne   How'd the check go then?

Jen *shoots a look at* **Stacey**. **Jen***'s a terrible liar.* **Stacey**, *on the other hand . . .*

Stacey   Oh yeh, we're right as rain. We don't get up to any of that.

A beat. **Stacey** *knows she needs to change the subject.*

Stacey   This is what I love about you, Leanne, we can chat to you about owt. I wish it was like that at mine. Dad's . . . well, he's Dad . . . and I can't get a word in edgeways with Mam, between 'Where's my book bag?', 'Mum, there's no milk in!', 'Muuum, Jay's shat on the floor again and he's eating it!'

Leanne   Your mam loves you dearly, pet.

Stacey   I know, it's just, you two are so close, I wish I had that.

Jen (*with love*)   Most of the time she just pesters me until I pay attention. She's like a fly.

Leanne (*whilst playfully jabbing* **Jen**)   Bzzz. Bzzz. Bzzz.

They all start buzzing at each other and playfighting. They chase one another out of the room.

Scene Three: Club Toilet

A Thursday. A week before Christmas. Club Ocean. We can hear a remix version of Mariah Carey's 'All I Want for Christmas Is You' in the background. The two girls squeeze into a tiny toilet cubicle and close the door behind themselves.

Stacey   Lock's fucked.

Jen   I'll hold it wi' me arse.

Stacey   Ta. Here, hold my purse while I just –

Stacey *passes her purse to* **Jen**, *then pulls her dress up and hovers over the loo.*

Jen   Where'd you get this? Primani?

Stacey   Yeh, via Cancer Research. What do you reck?

Jen   S'alright. Didn't Elouise Jennings have one like that?

Stacey   Dunno.

Jen   Yeh, she did. Oh, hurry up will ya, I'm busting.

Stacey   Nearly done. Pass the bog roll.

Jen   All out. Have to shake.

Stacey   Fuck that. I'm not a skank! There's a pack of tissues in me bag, pass us one.

Jen *passes* **Stacey** *a tissue and* **Stacey** *wipes.*

Jen   Right, move over, if I sneeze, they'll be a wet patch.

Stacey *pulls her skirt down. They swap places.*

Stacey   Pretty sure you shouldn't be pissing yourself every time you sneeze, laugh or go on a trampoline.

Jen   Me mam does, just stick a fanny pad in, it's fine.

Stacey   I know, but can't you see a doctor for it or summat.

Jen   Gonna ask next week aren't I?

Stacey   Fair play. Jeez, Jen, your tits look massive from here. You on your period?

Jen   Nah, babe.

Stacey   I'm well jel. Mine are all – oh I don't know – far apart. I don't have a power cleavage like you. My left tit's over here like, 'Oi, right tit, come here, your tea's ready'. And my right tit is like, 'But I'm playing out, I'll be back in a bit'.

Jen   You're proper crackers you are.

Stacey   'Come back righty.' 'Noooooo . . .'

Jen   You know these aren't real don't you?

Stacey   You haven't had 'em done have ya?

Jen   No, you wally! You'd know if I had 'em done. You'd be holding me hand when I woke up post-op. I've just shoved a couple of fillets in me bra that's all.

Stacey   Fillet-O-Fish?

Jen   Chicken fillets. Primark's best. Two each side.

Stacey   Show us then.

Jen   Give us a sec.

Stacey gives **Jen** *a tissue,* **Jen** *wipes herself down then gets some hand sanitiser out, squirts it on both their hands and puts it away.*

Jen   Ladies and gentlemen, boys and girls, are you ready for the grand reveal?

Jen *produces one chicken fillet out of her bra in a playful showgirl style and then one from the other side.*

Jen   Now you see them . . .

She pulls out the other two chicken fillets.

Jen   Now you don't!

She tries to bow but it's too cramped.

Stacey   That's bloody witchcraft that is.

Jen   Great innit?

Stacey   Fucking marvellous. Oh, I gotta get me some of them.

Jen   £3 Primark. Double 'em up for maximum effect.

Stacey   I could get our Aidy to nick us some –

Jen   I can't imagine your brother's gonna be thrilled about having to slip some chicken fillets under his jacket for you to stuff in your bra . . .

Stacey   You take me to get some then. I'd be well embarrassed going on me own.

Jen   Here, have these.

Jen *hands* **Stacey** *two of the chicken fillets.*

Stacey   Nah, mate, it's cool.

Jen   Come on, button down ya top, I'll show you what to do.

Jen *begins to readjust* **Stacey**'s *boobs.*

Jen   You want to get it right underneath and angle it –

Female Voice (*from off*)   Is this one free?

Door opens a little bit but **Stacey** *shoves it back with her arse.*

Female Voice (*from off*)   Hurry up will ya, there's a massive bloody queue out here.

Jen   Piss off!

Female Voice (*from off*)   Don't be friggin' each other off in there.

Stacey   Be out in a sec!

Jen   Twats!

Stacey   So who you gonna pull tonight then?

Jen   Can't can I! Swore me oath of celibacy till I've sorted everything out down there.

Stacey   How long will that take?

Jen   Fuck knows, but it better not be long. I might seal up!

Stacey   You don't have to go the full way you know, could have a first base only rule.

Jen   Hmm . . .

Stacey   It's hard that though, because if you both get the frisk, you gotta come up with a reason why not . . . Guess you could say you're on.

Jen   Hmm . . .

Stacey   But for how long? I guess they'll be able to sort it pretty quick, this must happen all the time.

Jen   Hope so.

Stacey   Do you know who it was?

Jen   Nope.

Stacey   Not a clue?

Jen   Well, got an idea, but he swears it weren't him.

Stacey   How far back we talking?

Jen   Don't know for sure. Thinking two, maybe three. It's proper cringe to be honest. I texted Jonno first, he was a right dick about it.

Stacey   He's a dick full stop!

*Jen passes **Stacey** her phone to show her messages. **Stacey** reads the text aloud.*

Stacey   'Dirty fucking whore. Wouldn't dare get checked, if I get an itch, I'll tell every fucker you've got an infected fucking faj.' Charming!

Jen   If it gets out –

Stacey   Won't though, will it! Cos he'd have to admit he's been putting it about, and he's got that posh bird from St Margaret's on the go now.

Jen   I'm not going back to that school now, no chance.

Stacey   Don't worry, babe, two week off, it'll be old news by the time we get back.

Jen   When that video of Molly Papworth went round she was known as Snickers Girl for the rest of her life.

Stacey   A splash of the clap isn't half as bad as fingering yourself with a Snickers bar, don't get dramatic.

*Jen does the final adjustments on **Stacey**'s top.*

Jen   Fine. Right then you just rest 'em on top like that. And a bit of bronzer, just there . . .

*Jen takes a bronzer brush out her bag and contours **Stacey**'s cleavage.*

Jen   . . . and that will do the trick. Merry fucking Christmas!

*Jen squeezes **Stacey**'s new boobs before reinstalling two of her own chicken fillets. **Stacey** admires her new cleavage.*

Stacey   They're reunited!

Jen   Double up and they'll meet your chin for morning coffee!

Stacey   Thanks, babe, where would I be without you, eh?

Jen   Flat chested and frigid.

Female Voice (*from off*)   Are you done or what?

Jen   Who the fuck do you think you are?

Stacey   Coming out now!

Jen   No, we'll take as long as we fucking want. If you think –

Stacey (*distracting* **Jen** *to diffuse the situation*)   Bet you I can get the DJ to play 'Sexy Chick'!

Jen   You joking? He's a right grumpy bastard tonight. I've made three requests and he's completely blanked me. Fuck all festive cheer that one.

Stacey   Three shots says it's on before half past.

Jen   You're on!

Stacey   Ready to see the flutter in action?

They orientate themselves out of the tight cubicle. **Jen** *goes first.*

Jen (*to woman in queue*)   You wanna watch how you talk to folk.

Stacey *grabs* **Jen**'s *hand and leads her off.*

During the scene change we hear David Guetta's 'Sexy Chick' playing.

Scene Four: At the Clinic

The Tuesday after. Christmas Eve Eve. At the clinic. **Jen** *is behind the screen with the nurse wearing sarcastic reindeer deeley boppers.* **Stacey** *is sat uncomfortably on a chair in the main room.*

Nurse Just take off your underwear and lie down. Knees up.

Stacey *stifles a snigger.*

Jen (*trying to crack a joke*)   That's not the first time I've been told that!

Silence. **Nurse** *doesn't laugh.* **Stacey** *can't believe* **Jen** *would say something like that in a place like this.*

Jen   Sorry, inappropriate. It's just a little awkward is all . . .

Nurse   There's nothing to feel awkward about. This is my job. I've seen it all. Just relax.

Jen   Is it going to hurt?

Nurse   It might be slightly uncomfortable.

Stacey   That means it fucking kills, babe.

Jen   Oh fuck.

Nurse   Just relax.

Jen   After this will I be free?

Nurse   You'll be free to go home, yes.

Jen   No, free from . . . this.

Nurse   This is just a swab, so that we can run some further tests. I'll give you some antibiotics and that should clear things up for you.

Stacey   How long will this swab take?

Jen   Why, you got to be somewhere?

Stacey   Well, Mum says she's left tea in the microwave at home so if I don't get back before 7, it'll be devoured by the twins. It's a special tonight. Fish fingers, chips and beans.

Jen   I've got enough fish fingers going on here thanks very much.

Nurse   That's not entirely appropriate.

Jen   Neither's where you're shoving whatever the fuck that is, but I'm dealing with it aren't I?

Stacey   Is it in yet?

Jen   What?

Stacey   The swab thing.

Nurse   I'm inserting it now.

   Stacey *finds that word amusing.*

Stacey   So, you know you said you've seen it all . . . What's the weirdest thing you've seen?

Nurse   Patient confidentiality, I'm not allowed to say.

Stacey   Jen's mam once saw someone who'd tried to bleach their pubes but had an allergic reaction and it was all blistered and that.

Nurse   I'm sure that was very painful.

Jen   So what happens if people get more than one STI at once?

Nurse   We treat them for everything that we can treat them for.

Stacey   Jo from school said her cousin got syphilis from a toilet seat. Is she lying?

Nurse   Well, I don't know Jo or her poor cousin but that's pretty much impossible.

Jen   Told ya! You shouldn't believe anything Jo Mecklenburgh says cos she's a lying little bitch.

Nurse   I didn't say –

Stacey   If I get come in my eye, can I get hermes?

Jen   Herpes! You thick twat! And no, you can't –

Nurse   Well, actually you can . . .

Stacey   Ha! Now who's a thick twat?

Jen   At least I can tell a courier from a cold sore.

(*To the* **Nurse**.) Have you ever treat blue waffle?

Stacey   With ice cream?

Jen   And salty caramel sauce?

Stacey   And – [a chocolate flake]

Nurse (*shutting the blue waffle discussion down*)   Right, you're done. I'll send this off. Take these two tablets now and within twenty-four hours you should be right as rain; if you have any itchiness, come straight back. And to avoid spreading the infection further, don't have sexual intercourse for a week.

Jen   A week?

Nurse   Two weeks to be on the safe side.

Jen   Right.

Nurse   And you should encourage any current or recent sexual partners to have a test as well as they may have been infected. We can help you with this if you prefer.

Stacey   Awks.

Jen   No thanks.

Nurse   And you'll have to come back here for your tests from now on. It will clear up but it'll always be there, benign, so it shows up on the basic tests. Shall I send you an appointment?

Jen   Not yet.

Stacey   Can you hurry up, I'm gonna miss *Bake Off* at this rate.

Jen   Alright.

Jen emerges from the curtain pulling her pants up.

Jen   Cheers, Miss Nurse. Ta-ra.

They leave the clinic room holding hands.

Stacey   I hope you've got some hand sanitiser, you scruffy mare.

Jen   You can't catch it by holding hands. Can you?

Stacey   I dare you to go back and ask her.

Jen   I ain't stepping foot in there ever again. I think she's seen far too much of me and all.

They leave the clinic and start walking down the street.

Jen   Hey, you should've seen her face when I said blue waffle. What a picture!

Stacey   She wasn't having any of it!

Jen   Do you remember when Elouise went to the toilet in IT and you put that picture of blue waffle on her screen and then Mr Morrissey came to look at her work and got the full thing staring him right in the face.

Stacey   Course I remember.

Jen   I nearly took the rat for that.

Stacey   Good job Mr Morrissey can't say no to these puppy dog eyes, eh?

Jen   Aye.

Stacey   Isn't it wrap?

Jen   Isn't what rap?

Stacey   Took the wrap for that?

Jen   Beats me. Rat, wrap, rapping rats, makes no difference to me. Piss funny that – blue waffle.

Stacey   You're a blue waffle!

Jen   No you are.

Stacey   You are.

They exit, pushing and shoving at each other.

Scene Five: Rough Ride

January. First £1 Thursday of the year. 'We No Speak Americano' is playing in the background. Club Ocean toilets. **Stacey** *sits on the loo; she seems giggly and tipsy.* **Jen** *stands above.*

Stacey   Wee. Stop. Wee. Stop. Wee. Stop.

Jen   The fuck ya doing?

Stacey   Me pelvic flooring. Saw this video about a woman having six kids and she couldn't stop peeing ever! Cos she had bad pelvic flooring, so I'm doing this now. Wee. Stop. Wee. Stop. I thought with me mam having us five, it might run in the family.

Jen   Saggy flaps dunt run in the family, babe.

Stacey   It's not about your flaps, it's some muscles inside somewhere. You should try it, might mean you don't wet your pants when you sneeze.

Jen   That face you're making is great.

Stacey   What face?

Jen   This face.

   Jen *imitates* **Stacey***'s 'pelvic floor' face.*

Stacey   I don't look like that.

Jen   Do! I bet you can't do it to music.

Stacey   Bet I can. I'm expert me.

   Stacey *attempts to do her pelvic floor in time with the track that is playing in the background.*

Stacey   Shit me this is well hard.

> **Jen** *starts imitating her face again and taking the mickey out of her.* **Stacey** *starts laughing.*

Stacey   Don't make me laugh.

> **Stacey** *can't stop herself laughing and therefore no longer has control over her pelvic floor. They are both in stitches.*

Jen   See, told you, you couldn't do it.

Stacey   Bet I can when I'm sober!

Jen   Whatever! Ey, did you see Jack back there?

Stacey   Yeh, he looked well rough. What was he saying to you?

Jen   Said he's selling now. Asked if I wanted anything.

Stacey   I hope you said no.

Jen   Course I did. Can you imagine if my mam found out, with what she has to deal with at work?

Stacey   So how many you on then?

Jen   What about you?

Stacey   I asked first.

Jen   Including Jack, nine.

Stacey   Nine? Are you joking, I'm on eighteen! PB for me!

Jen   I'm not on top form. It's my downstairs disaster. It's ruined me.

Stacey   It's only pulling.

Jen   I know but I'm sure they can sense it. Like I'm plagued or summat.

Stacey   Hold on, are you including girls in your numbers?

Jen   Yeh.

Stacey   You can't do that! We didn't agree.

Jen   I saw you kiss Aisha.

Stacey   I know, but that's different . . .

Jen   Why is it different?

Stacey   Because I actually like girls like that.

Jen   So? If you're counting it, then I'm counting it. You want equality and everything, you can't have it both ways.

Stacey   Fair play. Still, if you don't kiss nine more people in the next eight minutes, I win and you've got to do five shots.

Jen   Five . . .

Stacey   I don't think I could do any more shots tonight. I necked three Jägerbombs just to face pulling Sam Wharley. He's the worst kisser . . .

   Jen *starts to look a bit worse for wear.*

Stacey   Adil has really stepped up his game though. I think he might be into me, he's giving it large.

   Stacey *gets up and sorts herself out.* **Jen** *is quiet.*

Stacey   And he's really fit. I think if I wasn't, like, where I'm at with Nathe, I'd definitely go there. Nathe told me that I'm the type of girl he falls for, you know. Got me this lipgloss for Christmas.

Jen   Nice.

Stacey   Thanks for the gentle encouragement, I guess I thought he was a bit out of my league, but he's really down to earth. We chat every day. He's always telling me how pretty I am, calls me his little poppet, won't let me pay for anything, says he just wants to look after me. I feel like a princess. And you were right, he's got lovely forearms! I saw him in his work clothes the other day and proper got the fanny flutters! It might be the Jägerbombs talking but I think I might be falling in love.

Jen   I'm gonna throw.

Stacey   Jen, don't be like that –

Jen   Move.

Jen shoves Stacey out the way and throws up into the toilets. It's a close call.

Stacey   Oh. You weren't joking. Right then.

Stacey takes a deep breath and tries to clear her head.

Stacey   Come on then, beauty queen, let's get that hair out of the way.

Stacey pulls Jen's hair and takes a hair clip from her own hair to hold it back. Stacey gets tissues from her bag and wipes Jen's mouth for her.

Stacey   That's right, get it all up. That came on a bit suddenly. I didn't even think you were that –

She is interrupted by Jen hurling again.

Stacey   Nice. I've never seen you eat carrots! You'll be rough at school tomorrow, tactical nap during UCAS class.

(*To outside the cubicle.*) Anyone got any water out there? My mate's a bit worse for wear.

Female Voice (*from off*)   Here.

A bottle of water flies over the top of the cubicle and nearly takes Stacey out.

Stacey   Watch it. Nearly took me clean out.

Female Voice (*from off*)   You're welcome.

Stacey   Here, Jen, have a sup of this, it'll make you feel better.

Jen swats the bottle away. Stacey gets an idea. She goes in Jen's bag and gets an Alka-Seltzer. She drops it in the bottle of water and shakes it up. As she takes the lid of the water, it fizzes everywhere.

Stacey   SHIT!

Male Voice (*from off*)   Everything alright in there?

Stacey   Yeh, everything's fine.

(*To herself.*) Come on, Stace, act sober. Act sober.

Male Voice (*from off*)   Are you doing drugs in there?

Stacey   No.

Male Voice (*from off*)   Is someone throwing up?

Stacey   She's just taking a moment.

  Jen *vomits loudly.*

Male Voice (*from off*)   If she's throwing up, I'm going to have to ask you to leave. You can't stay in there all night.

Stacey   It's fine, honestly.

Male Voice (*from off*)   Don't get cheeky, come on, out you come.

  Stacey *takes a deep breath, composes herself and turns on the innocent charm – she has done this sort of thing a thousand times before. She is in control now. She pokes her head out of the cubicle.*

Stacey   Look, sir, I don't mean to come across as cheeky, but my friend here has just had a really bad night. She's just seen her boyfriend of two years snogging another girl and he doesn't know that she's out tonight so she just needs a moment to compose herself before she goes back out there and confronts the cheating scumbag. If you could just give us five minutes, please, then I can restore her confidence, because she's honestly the most amazing girl I've ever met and doesn't deserve to be treat like that. Just five minutes please.

She flutters her eyelashes. He doesn't stand a chance against her puppy dog eyes.

Male Voice (*from off*)   Oh. Alright. Just don't linger about.

The bouncer walks away.

Jen (*head still in the toilet*)   Lies.

Stacey   Not all of it.

Jen   I want to go home.

Stacey   I'll come back to yours, I'll tell your mum that I'm not speaking to Dad again or something.

Jen   It's ok. I'll be fine, just put me in a taxi.

Stacey   I'm sticking with you, Jen. I'm always sticking with you.

They leave. 'I Don't Want to Miss a Thing' by Aerosmith plays.

Scene Six: Uni Open Day

A Tuesday late January. **Jen** *and* **Stacey** *are at a university open day in Newcastle. They walk around the campus with a flyer in their hand.*

Stacey   And this is where they all have their dinner.

Jen   Looks alright. Bet they don't do chips and curry sauce.

Stacey   Do on a Tuesday.

Jen   A Tuesday? Who eats chips and curry sauce on a Tuesday? Vom. Bet they don't have a £1 Thursday though, do they?

Stacey   Don't know yet.

Jen   Nowhere beats Ocean and their £1 Thursday! So what do you reckon then? You applying?

Stacey   I'd love to. Did you see them dancers? Like they were in their own little jewellery boxes.

Jen   Ballet looks a bit dross to me, but if you love it that much, you should put it down – top choice.

Stacey   But what do I do if I get in? Dad doesn't even know I'm here and you know how he feels about the whole thing. 'Uni's for posh folk, kid, it's nowt that a good graft can't teach ya. Can't you get yourself on one of them TV talent shows.'

Jen   You can't live your life doing what your dad wants, Stace. If you wanna do it, you gotta try. You can't wait around for permission because no one will give you it.

Stacey   No one's gonna give me the money for it either.

Jen   Didn't Mrs Jackson say she was helping you apply for a grant?

Stacey   She looked into it. There's nowt available anymore, people just gotta work out if they can stomach the debt.

Jen   You could just apply and see what happens.

Stacey   How? This finance form's got my head mashed.

Jen   Look, £8,944, they'll loan you that. That's about – nine grand over fifty – 180 a week. What's your digs? 100 max. Food £2 per meal. Seven by three that's twenty-one meals at – nah you'd have to do one fifty a meal. Then you're at about 132. Give yourself another twenty quid, say, for bills – phone and that. You're at £152 leaving you £28 for train home, spends and £1 Thursdays. Done.

Stacey   Apply with me?

Jen   What?

Stacey   Do your maths stuff here.

Jen   I don't even like maths.

Stacey   Think about the nights out. The freedom! We can go *oot on the toon* every week. Every day like a holiday! We could stay together, split us bills, you could cook Pot Noodle for tea.

Jen   I'm not sure, mate. They're not my type of people, you know that.

Stacey   But I'm your type of person, Jen, and I'm not applying if you don't apply with me – I need you.

Jen   Newcastle though?

Stacey   I can still teach up here because Tamsin has another branch of her dance school. You could keep her books or something.

Jen   If it makes you happy, I'll apply, but I'm not promising anything.

Stacey   We could start saving now. I'll need £60 for the train for the audition. We'll miss £1 Thursdays!

Jen   You can't miss this week! Zayn Malik's doing a guest appearance. I'll sub you. You can stay at mine and we'll share a taxi back. Or we could walk back, it's only about an hour ten to walk it, that's free. You can get drinks from folk when we're there. I can do my stealthy five-finger discount at the bar! Pre-drink at mine – Mam's got a bottle of dodge Lambrini that she won at the tombola at work. We could do this every week. Come on, please. I really need a drink. Please, Stace . . .

Stacey   I've got double sociology Friday . . .

Jen   What about Nathan? Isn't he coming out this week?

Stacey   Said he might be.

Jen   Well, you can't play hard to get forever you know.

Stacey   Go on then, but I need to be in bed by 3.

Jen   Done! We can celebrate being grown up and applying to uni.

Stacey   Deal.

Jen   Let's get out of here, stinks of old fanny.

Stacey   You'd know!

Jen   Watch it!

They link arms.

Stacey   You know they've got a Club Ocean in Newcastle.

Jen   Yeh, but I heard it's a fiver in.

Stacey   Not on student night. And they've got beds in the smoking area so you'll be right at home.

Jen   You're pushing it today, you are.

Stacey   No one would know you up here. You can leave all that other stuff behind.

Jen   Not really ever gone though, remember.

Stacey   Yeh, but –

Jen   I've said I'll apply, leave it at that. And you're having the aisle seat on way back, I'll chob if I've gotta do another two hour with Snotty Siddique.

   Stacey *is thrilled* **Jen**'s *applying – not thrilled about sitting next to Siddique.*

Act Two

Scene Seven: Well You Are a Slut –

*A Thursday. Early March. Music is generic thumping – the kind where all the songs sound the same. **Stacey** and **Nathan** are in an outdoor area of the nightclub.*

Nathan The way you dance up there. You blow me away.

Stacey The DJ rarely lets us up on the podium. I love it.

Nathan I couldn't take my eyes off you. No one could.

Stacey I'm thinking of going to dance college. You know, do it proper.

Nathan From what I can see, there's nothing anyone can teach you.

*Suddenly **Stacey** is snogging **Nathan**'s face off. **Jen** appears and stands awkwardly on her own, holding a drink.*

Jen Stace?

Stacey (*whilst kissing*) Mhm?

Jen It's getting late.

Stacey (*still kissing, it's inaudible*) Just a little bit longer.

Jen You said that half hour ago . . .

***Stacey** uses her hand, behind **Nathan**'s back, to waft **Jen** away. **Jen** walks off.*

Nathan You look so pretty tonight.

Stacey Shut up.

Nathan I've never met anyone like you.

Stacey You're too lovely.

Nathan Do you want to come back to mine?

Stacey   I don't know if I . . .

Nathan   You don't have to, don't feel pressured. We can take things at your pace. Whatever you're comfortable with.

Stacey   Thanks. Next time, I promise.

Nathan   I can't wait.

> **Nathan** *pulls her in and kisses her again.* **Jen** *returns; she's ready to go home.*

Jen   Come on, Cinderella, we're going.

Stacey (*still kissing* **Nathan**)   One minute.

Jen   I said, we're going!

> **Jen** *grabs* **Stacey** *and drags her off* **Nathan**. **Jen** *starts marching* **Stacey** *out of the club.* **Nathan** *tries to keep up.*

Stacey   Ow! What the fuck?

Jen   You said you wanted to be in bed by 3. Well, it's five to three, and we're walking back, so time to go.

Stacey   What?

Jen   We agreed.

Stacey   Nathan could drop us. Couldn't you, Nathe?

Jen   He's been drinking.

Stacey   So?

Jen   Come on, Stace – think about the jewellery box girls.

Stacey   I know but –

Jen   We've only spent £3.80. If we leave now, we're still on track.

Stacey   I don't know why you're always wanging on about this money thing, you don't even wanna go uni.

Jen   I just want you to be happy.

Stacey   No, you're jealous because I'm getting some and you're not.

Jen   What?

Nathan   Maybe it is time to be getting off . . .

Stacey (*to* **Nathan**)   But we've –

Jen   Spent the last forty minutes exchanging saliva, yes. Whilst I've frozen my tits off, had my arse grabbed four times and then been called a slut by Linzi Marsden from the year above.

Stacey   Well, you are . . .

Nathan   Stace.

Stacey   She is!

>   **Jen** *stops in her tracks. Even* **Nathan** *is taken aback by this.*

Jen   What?

Stacey   –

Jen   What did you just say?

Stacey   I didn't say nothing.

Nathan   Stacey, I really think –

Jen   What did you say?

Stacey   Nowt. Look, I was just saying, your tits might not be freezing off if they weren't practically out, that's all.

Jen   What the fuck, Stace? This is your top.

Stacey   Yeh but I don't wear it like that. Couldn't you have, I don't know, worn a cardi with it or summat?

Jen   Are you fucking joking? Have you seen yourself? This whole fucking club saw your arse when he slipped his old, wrinkly hands up your skirt just ten minutes ago.

Nathan   Sorry, what?

Stacey   Nathan, it doesn't matter.

(*Turns to* **Jen**.) He's not old, Jen, he's a real man! And anyway he's practically my boyfriend, so it might look slutty but it isn't. I'm not like you.

Jen   Are you shitting me right now?

Nathan   Come on, Jen, calm down. She doesn't mean –

Jen   No offence, Nathan, but this has nothing to do with you.

Stacey   I'm just saying that if maybe if you stuck to one guy and didn't flash your fanny for a drag on a fag then maybe Linzi Marsden wouldn't –

Jen   Fuck off.

> **Jen** *starts to walk away.* **Stacey** *perhaps realises this has gone a bit too far. She signals* **Nathan** *to stay where he is and follows* **Jen**.

Stacey   I didn't mean it like –

> **Jen** *wheels round again to face* **Stacey**.

Jen   How did you mean it then?

Stacey   Just –

Jen   Go on.

Stacey   . . .

Jen   You just called me a slut!

Stacey   But, I –

Jen   No, Stace. You don't get it. You don't get to call me that. They can say what they want. Jonno can call me whatever. Fucking Linzi Marsden, Mr Jackson, even bleeding Nathan, they can say whatever the fuck they want. But you, you don't dare say that to me. It's a dirty, dirty word. Five years I've known you, Stacey Blackwell, and I've never judged you once. Never. Five fucking years! Who the fuck do you think you are to say that to me? I'm not a fucking walking vagina!

Jen *is done. She storms off in her heels; she isn't completely steady on her feet.* **Stacey** *follows again.* **Jen** *doesn't turn now.*

Stacey   Jen, wait up.

Jen   FUCK YOU!

Jen *want to be strong, but she is cut deep.*

Stacey   Jen!

Jen *continues walking off and flicks the finger at* **Stacey** *as she does.* **Stacey** *is stood alone for a second; she realises she's done wrong.* **Nathan** *joins her and puts his arm round her. He tries to kiss her but she's not feeling it anymore. He tries harder; she literally has to recoil to escape it. He pulls her head in to rest on his chest and kisses her forehead. He walks her off.*

The thumping music fades.

Scene Eight: How Am I Going to Pay for That?

A week later. Thursday. 7 p.m. **Leanne**, **Jen**'s *mum, enters her kitchen. She is looking for something and tidying as she goes along – pottering and faffing.*

Leanne   Phone. Phone. Phone. I went . . . through to . . . rang Daryll, then did . . . then what? Think. Think. Think.

She gets her bag out and looks through it.

Keys. Diary. EpiPen. Atkins bar – don't know how long that's been in there. Hair clip. Receipt – Pizza Express – from March, last year. Bloody hell, Leanne, sort your life out.

She bins the receipt. She starts to walk out but then turns around and walks back in.

Texted Jen for milk, was folding the – TABLETS.

She opens numerous medicine bottles and takes a tablet from each. Fills a glass of water and swallows the tablets. She goes to leave the room, forgets where she is going, stops herself, then remembers and leaves the room.

Leanne *re-enters with a pile of post. She opens the letters.*

Leanne (*reading*)   Twats! £200 a year. How much more do you want? Shirt off me bleeding back? You only collect my bin every chuffing fortnight, you robbing bastards.

She sees a letter; it stops her in her tracks. It's not addressed to her. She investigates the letter. She won't open the letter but she holds it up to the light. She tries to gently open it without tearing. She holds it over the steam of the kettle to open it.

Sound of the front door opening.

Jen (*offstage*)   Heyyy!

Leanne puts the letter on the table quickly and tries to busy herself. Jen enters.

Leanne   Hi, love. Good day?

Jen   Yeh. Y'alright?

Leanne   Lost my bleeding phone again haven't I?

Jen   Shall I ring it?

Leanne   It's on silent.

Jen   Did you set up 'Find my Phone'?

Leanne   I didn't understand it.

Jen   It's proper easy.

Leanne   You said you'd do it for me.

Jen   No, I didn't.

Leanne   Well, will you?

Jen   Yeh, when you find it.

Jen picks up the letter, takes one look and starts to leave.

Leanne   So . . . what did you do today then?

Jen   Not much.

Leanne   What you doing tonight?

Jen   Nowt.

Leanne   Not going out?

Jen   No.

Leanne   You and Stace –

Jen   No. Haven't you got evening class tonight?

Leanne   Yeh. It's a guest speaker tonight, fella from the boxing gym.

Jen   Oh yeh. Self-defence or summat was it?

Leanne   Yeh. But, I mean, you and I could, you know, hang out – if you fancied it?

Jen   Are you feeling alright, Mam?

Leanne   Right as rain love, why?

Jen   Well, you were right looking forward to the boxing thing. Said the instructor was six foot three and built like a brick shit house.

Leanne   Yeh but, I mean, work and – if you're not – well, I miss you is all.

Jen   What?

Leanne   We haven't hung out in ages.

Jen   We watched *Corrie* and had tea last night.

Leanne   I know, but . . .

Jen   What's this about?

Leanne   Nothing?

Jen   Are you taking your meds?

Leanne   Yes! And it's just bleeding Sertraline, everyone's on it these days. Don't try getting me sectioned for wanting to spend some time with you.

Jen *looks at the letter in her hand and clicks.*

Jen   Have you been snooping at my stuff again?

Leanne   What?

Jen   This. Is this what all this is about?

Leanne   I don't snoop! I didn't snoop!

Jen   Pfft.

Leanne   I was just looking for my phone . . .

Jen   In my post?

Leanne   It came through my letterbox, so when you pay the fucking council tax you can – Open it then!

Jen *opens the letter and reads it.*

Jen   It's nothing.

Leanne   Doesn't look like nothing to me.

(*Takes letter and reads it.*) An interview? University? Maths?!

Jen   It was just –

Leanne   Our Helen said there was a job cleaning at St Paul's kids' school, which I can fit around the surgery. Then I can save –

Jen   Mam, I'm not saying –

Leanne   It's just with the fridge packing in, it's set me back.

Jen   Mam –

Leanne   I was getting a hold of things, I was –

Jen   Mam –

Leanne   And I know I need to be better and I will, I will. I'll –

Jen   Mam, will you just fucking listen to me for a second.

Leanne   –

Jen   I don't want to go to Newcastle, I fucking hate maths. It was Stacey's idea. It's not exactly me, is it?

Leanne   It could be you love, if that's what you want.

Jen   I don't know what I want to be honest, I just want to live and find out along the way, you know.

Leanne   I'm sorry, love . . . that I can't give you more.

Jen   Mam, you give me every penny you have and work all hours God sends to keep a roof over my head. There's people at that school that treat families like us as a statistic, I'm a box to be ticked. Get a token poor kid into uni, that'll do the trick.

   Jen *is tidying up as she speaks.*

Jen   Here's your phone. Behind the bread bin.

Leanne   Fucking menopause!

Jen   Why've you got a missed call from Stacey?

Leanne   She fancies a drink and wants to meet you in town.

Jen   Why is she calling you?

Leanne   Because you don't answer.

Jen   I was mad.

Leanne   I know. Are you still?

Jen   Don't know.

Leanne   When shall I pack your bags for university then?

Jen   Not yet. I need a bit of time. To process.

Leanne   You've got all the time in the world, love.

Jen   You haven't. Self-defence starts in five.

Leanne   Looking after you always comes before looking after myself, you know that.

Jen   Ta, Mam. Now will you just go to boxing please, I've embarrassed myself.

Leanne   Not until you say you love me.

Jen   Don't be daft.

Leanne   Say it, or I'll stay here all night and cramp your style with my menopausal ways.

Jen   I love you, Mam.

Leanne   Sorry I didn't quite hear that.

Jen   I'm not saying it again. Get yourself to self-defence, Boxing whatever. And don't cringe yourself out by flirting outrageously with Mr Six Foot Three.

Leanne   Never! You know I'll always back your corner don't you, sweetheart. I'll be ringside every step of the way.

    Leanne *fake shadow boxes at* **Jen**.

Jen   Go!

Leanne   Bye, love. You think on that letter, Jennifer, could be good for you. First Mason to make summat of us-selves.

    Leanne *goes to leave*.

Jen (*calling after her*)   Mum! Water bottle!

    Jen *hands her the water bottle*.

Leanne   Fucking menopause.

Jen   Love ya, Mam. And hey, if you're not in bed by twelve, come home!

    Leanne *leaves.* **Jen** *takes out a phone. She is undecided. She leaves the room.*

Scene Nine: Last £1 Thursday

Same evening. 11 p.m. **Stacey** *is stood outside Club Ocean with* **Nathan**. *Sound of an engine ticking over.*

Nathan   I thought you said your mates were already here.

Stacey   They will be any minute.

Nathan   I'll wait with you till they arrive.

Stacey   Honestly, you don't have to.

Nathan   I don't mind.

Stacey   You've got work in the morning.

Nathan   I'll be fine. Who's out again?

Stacey   Some girls you don't know.

Nathan   Who?

Stacey   What does it matter?

Nathan   I'm just interested is all.

Stacey   Girls from school. Sarah-Jane and that.

Nathan   Cool. What time you gonna be back?

Stacey   I don't know, 3, maybe 4 if we go to Mode.

Nathan   That's a bit late.

Stacey   It's a girls' night.

Nathan   Why don't I pick you up at 1 then you can save the taxi home?

Stacey   Honest, it's fine.

Nathan   You've got to save for your big business plan. Taxi to mine will be pricey at 3.

Stacey   I'll text you at half one. Let you know what's going on.

Nathan   Ok. Make sure you do.

Stacey   I'm gonna head in now.

Nathan   But they're not here yet?

Stacey   They're probably already in there – they wouldn't want to miss the £1 entry!

Nathan   Ok, then, my little poppet, but you take care won't you, and call me if you need anything.

Stacey   Will do.

Nathan   Don't I get a kiss?

> **Nathan** *strokes her hair and gives her a gentle kiss on the forehead.*

Stacey   You don't have to worry so much you know. I'm an adult.

Nathan   Not technically.

Stacey   Yeh, ok, but –

Nathan   I love you.

Stacey   Love you too. See ya!

> **Nathan** *exits reluctantly.* **Stacey** *waltzes towards the Club Ocean queue. She looks around. No one is there. It's not quite the same being on her own. She realises how alone she is without* **Jen***. Being alone is her biggest fear. She considers leaving.* **Jen** *enters.*

Jen   Oi. Wait up.

> **Stacey***'s relieved. She gives* **Jen** *a massive hug, then remembers that they haven't been speaking and awkwardly lets go.*

Stacey   I didn't know if you'd –

Jen   Well, I did.

Stacey   I'm glad.

Jen   I shouldn't have lost it.

Stacey   Are you joking? Yes, you should. I was bang out of order. I didn't mean what – I was just with Nathe and then I'd had too much and things got out of hand. Then when you didn't show at school, I was worried, so I texted your mam. She said you didn't want to hear from me and I thought – well, I don't know what I thought, I just thought maybe that was it for us and – I'm sorry.

Jen   It for us? Bit dramatic, babe.

Stacey   But your mum –

Jen   Well, she was right, I was fuming. Didn't want to speak to you. But now I'm over it. So it's fine.

Stacey   You didn't need to slam school.

Jen   No way I'm going in when everyone including you thinks I'm a whore.

Stacey   I don't –

Jen   I know but I was being a mardy stubborn bitch so kicked off a bit. Over it now.

Stacey   I really am sorry.

Jen   I know, stop banging on about it.

Stacey   And I actually think that you're really inspiring, the way that you're sexually liberated and that. I'm mean, it's okay for lads to be so why shouldn't –

Jen   Alright, that's enough, I'm done with this conversation. You're forgiven. Let's move on.

Stacey   Drink?

> **Stacey** *pulls two small miniature vodka bottles that you'd get at airports out of her bag; they are filled with a murky liquid. She passes one to* **Jen**.

Jen   The fuck is this?

Stacey   No vodka left at home, so I made a Stacey Special.

Jen Oh frig. What's in it?

Stacey Owt from the cupboard.

Jen I'm gonna feel this in the morning.

They both cheers and neck their drinks. It tastes rough, and burns.

Stacey Ooo . . . Can you taste the eggnog?

Jen I can't taste anything ever again.

Stacey More?

Stacey *produces two more bottles of the murky liquid and they both neck them as well.*

Stacey Are you shitting it . . . about the whole leaving home thing?

Jen Dunno.

Stacey I am.

Jen You practically do everything on your own already, Stace, you're the most independent person I know.

Stacey And what about Nathan?

Jen How's that going?

Stacey Yeh, great. Stay at his most nights now. Told Dad I'm at yours. It's lovely actually, I feel really settled there.

Jen That's lush.

Stacey And he's really supportive with everything. Thinks I need to be putting more time into my teaching. Says maybe I should try to go out a little less, you know, so I can start building a little business out of it.

Jen You're gonna be up there though, in Newcastle, doing it proper, for yourself.

Stacey I know, but you have to be really good, Jen, and I've not done classes or owt.

These aren't **Stacey**'s *words.* **Jen** *doesn't quite know where this has come from.*

Jen   You're ten times better than any of them, babe.

Stacey   It's just . . .

Jen   Stace, are you ok?

Stacey   Yeh, I'm great.

Jen   You seem a bit . . .

Stacey   I'm really good, honest.

Jen   You're not off with me are you?

Stacey   Not at all.

Jen   What is it then?

Jen *can tell that* **Stacey** *isn't quite 100 per cent but* **Stacey** *is giving nothing away.*

Stacey   It's nothing, I'm really happy at the minute, and now, with you, it's just so great to be speaking again. I proper miss you.

Jen   Don't be so soft. Have another drink.

Stacey *gets a larger water bottle out of her bag; it's a wonder how she fits everything in there. The bottle is filled with the murky liquid. They take turns on having swigs from it.*

Jen   It's not actually that bad when you get used to it.

Stacey   Did you hear, that guy from *Geordie Shore* is doing a guest appearance here on a £1 Thursday in October.

Jen   Which one?

Stacey   I think it's the first Thursday or summat.

Jen   I meant which guy, you doilum!

Stacey   The fit one. The mega-fit one. Adam.

Jen   You joking? I can't wait.

Stacey   We'll be at uni though won't we?

Jen   We'll come back. I don't care. We aren't missing it, no chance. He gives me the full fanny flutter!

Stacey   I bloody love you. Come on, let's go in.

Jen *and* **Stacey** *enter Club Ocean.*

Dance sequence to Katy B, 'Get Low' by Lil Jon and The East Side Boyz, 'Sak Noel' by Loca People.

Stacey *and* **Jen** *have a routine for every single song. The swish, dip, pout and slut drop from earlier is included. They may encourage/flirt with the audience to join in. The whole theatre should feel like a proper banging nightclub.*

Stacey *clearly has a raw talent that she would never see.*

The lights snap change and suddenly we are back outside the nightclub on the same night. **Jen** *and* **Stacey** *have been forced out of Club Ocean; they've had an altercation with the bouncers.* **Jen** *is kicking off.*

Jen   Cunts.

Stacey (*shouting off*)   Don't touch what you can't afford, mate.

(*To* **Jen**.) I can't believe that.

Jen   And I nearly pulled Stefan!

Stacey   He's fit.

Jen   So fit.

Stacey   So fucking fit.

Jen   Tonight was my chance with him.

Stacey   There's always Saturday.

Jen   £3 a drink and a fiver entry, don't think so.

Stacey   Fair point.

Jen   I want a night out, not a fucking mortgage.

Stacey   You sound like your mam.

Jen   Don't.

Stacey   I can't believe this.

Jen   Tonight was gonna be our night.

Stacey   I know.

Jen   And I'm busting for a piss.

Stacey   Now you mention it, I need a waz too. What about Revs?

Jen   It shut at 1.

Stacey   There's Lipstick.

Jen   It's halfway across town and if I walk another step in these New Look shoes, I think these blisters might actually get married and have two kids of their own.

Stacey   What about over there?

Jen   Don't be a skank.

Stacey   Needs must though.

Jen   I know but –

Stacey   Boys do it –

Jen   I guess so.

Stacey   Just squat, it's fine.

Jen   But I'm wearing a playsuit.

Stacey   You'll just have to pull it to one side.

Jen   And hope for the best?

Stacey   Pray for no spray.

Jen   Oh fuck it.

Jen *and* **Stacey** *giggle and run over to a slightly concealed corner, still very visible to the street.*

Jen   Show us then.

Stacey   Well, you just sorta squat like this, and then go. Try to get your legs as wide as possible and if you tilt your hips you can sort of try aim it.

Jen   Playsuit to one side. Check.

Stacey   Nice knicks.

Jen   Asda. Pound.

Stacey   Bargain.

Jen   Right, tilt hips forward.

Stacey   And go.

Jen   You first.

Stacey   You're the one that's busting, I can hold it for a bit longer.

Jen   Nah, I'm alright me.

Stacey   Right, after three.

Jen/Stacey   One . . . two . . . three . . .

Jen *and* **Stacey** *are both squatting and pissing against the wall.*

Jen   I'm aiming it! I'm aiming it!

Stacey   Don't splash us, you skank!

They finish pissing.

Jen   Fuck, I needed that. Giz a tissue.

Stacey, *still in squat, starts trying to root through her 'going out' bag.*

Stacey   I'm out.

Jen   We used mine earlier to wipe the loo seats down.

Stacey   It's fine, just shake.

Jen   Fuck off.

　　Stacey *starts shaking and* **Jen** *copies.*

Jen   It doesn't even feel dry though.

Stacey   You'll be alright, just use your knicks to mop it up and throw 'em in the wash when you get home.

They both readjust their clothing and stand up. **Jen** *gets out her hand sanitiser and they both wash their hands with it.* **Jen** *looks at the hand sanitiser then at her downstairs.*

Stacey   Don't, it'll burn like a bitch.

Jen   Hm. Fair. I've had enough burning sensations up there for the time being thank you very much.

They both look at each other and burst out laughing; they can't hold themselves up they're laughing that much. They seem like they're pulling it together but then crease up again.

They start to stagger back to the club.

Stacey   Can't believe you've never pissed outside before.

Jen   I'm not some sort of skank.

Stacey   But you've had sex outside.

Jen   Yeh, but that's different. And, well, needs must.

Stacey   I love you.

Jen   Don't get all soppy on me now just cos I've pissed in the street.

Stacey   Jen, where we going? They won't let us back in Ocean.

Jen   Oh shit. Well, I can't be arsed going to Lipstick, it's too far.

Stacey   And it's tenner entry at this time, it's a joke.

Jen   Guess we better get a taxi then.

Stacey   Yeh.

A pause.

Stacey   I don't really want to go home yet.

Jen   No, me neither.

Stacey   Nowhere to go though.

Jen   That kerb looks comfy.

Stacey   Alright.

The girls go sit on the edge of a kerb.

Stacey *gets another little bottle of alcohol from her bag; they each swig from it.*

Jen   What's this one, Mary Poppins?

Stacey   Sixty-five per cent rum from me dad's cupboard, tastes like shit but gets you fucked well fast. Supercalifragilistic-let'sgetfucked-ioutious

Jen *takes another swig.*

Jen   I'm glad we come tonight you know.

Stacey   Me too.

A pause.

Stacey   Nathe says you're no good for me.

Jen   Well, he can fuck off then can't he?

Stacey   He just – I don't know – he doesn't get it, I guess.

Jen   Look, babe, I don't care what he thinks. I just want to enjoy tonight. We're starting exams and then uni and things are gonna be different, but that's just life innit. So let's just live for right now. Yeh?

Stacey   Yeh.

A pause. **Stacey** *has something to say.*

Stacey   Has any lad ever, like, you know, hit you?

Jen   Like in a row?

Stacey   Well, yeh . . .

Jen   You know my ex Carl, he pulled a knife on me once, he thought I was cheating, saw red, next thing I know, he's got a varicose vein in his forehead and he's coming at me with the bread knife.

Stacey   Jeez.

Jen   It was pretty intense.

Stacey   I'm not sure if it's right you know . . .

Jen   Maybe. I guess some guys are just like that.

Stacey   I guess . . .

A pause.

Stacey   Rum?

Jen   Yeh, it's good this stuff, warms you right up.

Stacey   Hey, next time you're planning on sitting on the street corner all night, let me know, and I'll bring a jacket.

Jen *playfully shoves* **Stacey**, *they smile at each other. 'Angels' by Robbie Williams can be heard blaring from Club Ocean.*

Jen   What a way to spend our last £1 Thursday before exams.

Stacey   Doesn't have to be the last.

Jen   We've got to save for Newcastle.

Stacey   Yeh. We'll still have an amazing summer though, won't we? We can grab some White Lightning and go down Harold Park. And we can go off and do whatever we want, sticking to the budget. It's literally gonna be the best. I'm buzzing for it.

Jen   Yeh. Me too.

She looks out to the audience.

Hey, look, it's Ocean's very own Party Paul!

(*Calls over.*) Y'alright, Paul? Happy fiftieth! Get home safe, lad!

Stacey   Jeez, I hope I'm not here when I'm fifty.

Jen   On this kerb?

Stacey   No, here, Bradford.

Jen   What's wrong with Bradford?

Stacey   Nowt as such, but don't you just sometimes feel sort of stuck?

Jen   What's wrong with being stuck?

Stacey   Take our Aidy, he's nearly twenty-four, and what's he got for it? He good at nicking stuff but he hasn't ever been out of Bradford, probably never will.

Jen   And?

Stacey   I don't know it's just, I want to have my shit together. Know what I'm doing with my life, have a path or some shit to follow. I can't just chug along and go wherever the wind takes me.

Jen   I can. Newcastle, London, America. You can go anywhere, it's still the same old shit. People just getting by, in any way they know how. But I tell you what they don't have, they don't have a £1 Thursday!

Stacey   There's more to life than a £1 Thursday.

Silence. Maybe she's right. Maybe she's not.

Jen   Well, you won't have to put up with it forever. You've got the dance course starting soon, you can get yourself out of Bradford and kiss this sorry kerb goodbye.

Stacey   I didn't make it, Jen.

Jen   What?

Stacey   The audition. I couldn't get there – me and Nathe – we had a row and –

Jen   Are you fucking kidding?

Stacey   I'm sorry – I –

Jen   I think it's time I was getting off.

> **Jen** *gets up and goes to leave. There's no acid in what she says, she just knows it's the end of a chapter.* **Stacey** *might cry. Robbie Williams's 'Angels' fades in the background. Enter* **Nathan**.

Stacey   What are you doing here?

Nathan   I was worried about you.

Stacey   I texted, I'm fine.

Nathan   You're sat on a kerb.

Stacey   Sorting out my shoes.

Nathan   Where's your friends?

Stacey   One of them threw up so they went home.

Nathan   So you're on your own?

Stacey   Jen's here. She's just nipped to the loo . . .

(*Lie.*) We look after each other, you know.

Nathan   Right. I just worry, when it's only the two of you. What if she goes off with some guy?

Stacey   She wouldn't leave me on my own.

Nathan   You don't know that.

Stacey   I do.

Nathan   Look love, I don't want to argue. We talked about this. Why don't you come back to mine, then I can drop you off bright and early for your exam in the morning? It's 2 a.m., if we head home now you'll still get a good five hours' rest.

Stacey   But what about Jen?

> **Jen** *returns; she's clocked* **Nathan**'s *van and comes back. She gives* **Stacey** *a look that says 'I've got your back here'.*

Jen   Hey, Nathan, y'alright? Stace didn't tell me you were coming out.

Nathan   I'm not.

Jen   Right.

Nathan   I'm taking Stace home, she's got her exam in the morning and it's getting late.

Jen   It's only 2.

Nathan   Well, she didn't really want to come out anyway so –

Jen   She asked –

Stacey   It is getting pretty late, maybe it's –

Jen   Nathan, why don't you hang about and have a drink?

Nathan   I'm driving. Come on, Stacey.

Stacey   Can we drop Jen off on the way home?

Nathan   I'd love to but I've brought the van so there's only one seat.

Stacey   But we can't leave her by herself.

Nathan   She'll probably want to stay here and, you know, find a stranger to finger her or something.

Jen   What?

Stacey   Don't say that, Nathan.

Nathan I was only joking. It's banter. Look, it doesn't matter. Come on, Jen, you'll be alright getting a taxi won't you?

Jen Yeh, I'll be fine, but – Stace, are you sure you want to get off?

Nathan (*to* **Jen**) Haven't you got to revise tomorrow or summat? Come on, Stacey love, I can't be parked long cause I'm in a loading bay.

> **Nathan** *steers* **Stacey** *towards the van.* **Jen** *follows.*

Jen Stace, aren't you going to say bye?

Nathan I'll get you a coat, you say your goodbyes. Good to see you, Jen, get home safe.

> **Nathan** *goes to get a coat from the back of the van. The girls hug.*

Jen (*in* **Stacey**'s *ear*) You don't have to go if you don't want to.

Stacey He's just looking out for me. I'm sorry. Just leave it now please.

Jen Come to mine and we'll work it out.

Stacey I can't. It's done. Leave it.

> **Nathan** *comes back and puts a coat around* **Stacey**'s *shoulders.*

Nathan There you are, love, I've put the heated seats on for you.

Stacey Bye, Jen.

> **Stacey** *gets in the van. We may be able to see her sat in the passenger seat. She would be able to hear, but she wouldn't say a thing.*

Nathan What has she had to drink?

Jen Barely anything.

Nathan She looks pretty hammered to me.

Jen   I've seen her hammered, a lot. She's fine.

Nathan   You should be more responsible, you know she can't handle her drink.

Jen   I wouldn't let anything happen to her.

Nathan   It's alright for you, pissed all the time, still ace all your exams. It's not like that for her, she's got these pipe dreams and soon enough reality'll come crashing down and she needs a back-up plan or she'll be back in that fucking chaos of a family.

Jen   If you'd actually took her to the audition like you said you would, she might achieve her 'pipe dreams' but that's far too fucking scary for you, innit?

Nathan   Can't you see you're different? You're not like us. You'll go away, get new mates, have a great fucking life and I'll be left to pick up the pieces.

Jen   You don't know the first fucking thing about me.

Nathan   I know you won't be eighteen forever. It's time you grew the fuck up! Get a taxi, go home.

He throws some money at her feet, gets into his van and drives off. **Jen** *is stood on the pavement, in her tiny skirt with money at her feet and tears in her eyes.*

Jen   See you around, Stacey Blackwell.

Jen *looks at herself. She wraps her arms around herself, leaves the money and walks home.*

Scene Ten: Is This a Bit of Me?

Jen *enters a room with a desk where a man with beige trousers and a top-knot sits on the other side.* **Jen** *is out of her comfort zone and has overdressed to make up for it. Some might say there's a nudge too much tit for an interview.*

Jen   Hi.

Tristan   Jennifer?

Jen   It's Jen.

Tristan   Take a seat.

Jen   Thanks.

Tristan   I'm Tristan.

We know what **Jen** *thinks of his name.*

Tristan   So, why maths?

Jen (*blag*)   I've always loved maths, the challenge of it, problem solving, you know, numbers . . .

Tristan   And you're predicted a C currently.

Jen   Yeh . . . but the teacher's – [a cunt]. I'll get an A.

Tristan   That's a large jump in grades at A Level.

Jen   I'll do it.

Tristan   Fair enough. And what attracts you to higher education? It says in your personal statement that you're the first in your family to apply – is that right?

Jen   Yeh. It is. The nightlife sounds like a laugh.

Tristan *is shocked but amused.*

Jen   Only messing. I'd just love to expand me mind, you know. I think it's important. Opens a lot of doors, doesn't it, for the future. I heard that you've got to have a degree to join the dole queue these days.

Tristan (*ignoring the dole comment*)   It's true, there's a lot of opportunities for those who decide to further their education. Do you have an idea about where you'd like to go after university?

Jen   Home probably.

Tristan   With your career?

Jen   I'd like to figure that out you know, through the course.

Tristan   This is pure maths, not applied.

Jen   Yeh but you could do a bit of, like, coaching and that on potential careers during?

Tristan   It's not the main focus –

Jen   Why not? What's the use in letters after your name if they don't spell owt for your future.

Tristan   A lot of people pursue academia just for the love of it.

Jen   What?

Tristan   You might choose to stay and study a master's or a PhD.

Jen   Calm down – if I even do uni it'll be a means to an end. Not dragging it on for ten years or nowt. I'd be, like, twenty-seven when I get out. You should have your shit together by then.

Tristan   I wish. Do you have any questions?

Jen   That referencing stuff? I won't need that in maths will I?

Tristan   You'll be expected to explore case studies and methodologies.

Jen   Why though?

Tristan   Because that's what academia is.

Jen   I just think that sometimes things could benefit from a new way of thinking, you know that's relevant, not old and stuffy.

Tristan   I'm inclined to agree but that's not really the way it works.

Jen   It should be.

Tristan Perhaps.

Jen If you're always looking back then you're not really looking forward, and if you want to progress you have to think outside the box.

Tristan Perhaps you'd like to consider the philosophy courses, or something like business management or politics. You could even do a joint honours if you wanted?

Jen No offence but there ain't no way I'm gonna be a politician – they dress like shit and pretend they're something that they're not and I won't do that. Ever.

Tristan I can see that.

Jen You think I'm a tramp don't you?

Tristan Not at all.

Jen You do. I can see it, the way you look at us. I knew you'd be like this. Stuck-up and as beige as your pants.

Tristan Are you done?

Jen I'm sure I've got more in me.

Tristan I'm sure you have too but before you insult my choice of tie, let me ask you if you know a place called Little Horton?

Jen In Bradford? Course.

Tristan Ten years ago, I was living there with my dad in a two-bed terrace.

Jen You're too posh for Little Horton.

Tristan And now I'm studying for a doctorate whilst teaching.

Jen You've done well for yourself. Sold your soul a bit, cos there's not a sniff of Bradford on you.

Tristan I visit my dad once a fortnight, take him for a curry.

Jen   You still visit Bradford?

Tristan   Of course.

Jen   Oh. Right. Bet you think I'm a bit of twat then, saying that about your trousers.

Tristan   I think you could watch your mouth a bit, and you'll learn that, but I also want to push your application through and make sure you get an unconditional offer on maths and politics, or pure maths if you think you're up for it.

Jen   Why?

Tristan   Because you're different, Jen, and this uni, this world, needs a bit of different.

Jen   That's kind of you. Really, but truth is – this uni stuff it costs a fortune and people like me, I'm not like you. This lad at work, right, he went to uni, got himself about £50k of debt and now he's shelf stacking with me. And the manager – who hasn't got all his teeth let alone a GSCE – just talks to him like shit. Why would I spend £50k to go back to stacking? That's almost an 'ole house where we're from. No mortgage, nowt.

Tristan   What is it that you want, Jen?

Jen   Sorry?

Tristan   If you could have anything –

Jen   I can't have –

Tristan   Before you shut me and my beige trousers down again, let's just play make-believe for a second – What is it that you most want? Anything.

A pause.

Jen   Me mam to not have to work. And a new phone cos mine's shit.

Tristan   Ok, well, let's say your mum's outgoings to live nicely are £20k a year: rent –

Jen   I'd love her to own her own place, you know. Have something they can't take off her.

Tristan   Great, so mortgage, a monthly pedicure –

Jen   Self-defence classes.

Tristan   Everything. To give up work she'd need £20k in spare cash a year. Let's also say that you choose pure maths here and you really apply yourself, and you get in the top per cent of your class. You graduate from here with an offer from a credit card company or some banking firm and you could be earning £40k a year, first year out of uni.

Jen   Nah. That's proper balling that.

Tristan   You're five years out of uni, the boss loves your work and your charisma – don't fight me on this – your charisma is endearing and everyone enjoys working with you, so at your yearly appraisal, he –

Jen   Or she!

Tristan   Or she – offers you a promotion, move to the London office –

Jen   Fuck off.

Tristan   Fine, move to the Manchester office and you'll be on £70k a year, company car.

Jen   Leather seats?

Tristan   If that's what you wanted. And guess what after tax which is roughly 30 per cent all in –

Jen   50k.

Tristan   Yeh. 50k. Cash. Yours. Every year.

Jen   20 for mum.

Tristan   And 30 for you to do whatever you want with.

Jen   That's like half a house.

Tristan   Every year.

Jen   This is bullshit.

Tristan   It doesn't even end there. Many people in high finance jobs earn over 100 grand a year in their thirties.

Jen   Are you gonna earn 100 grand when you're thirty?

Tristan   I'm doing a PhD so it's different.

Jen   So it's lies then. You're trying to sell me some big wham bam – look at what you could've won – dream, when you're sat there and you don't have a pot to piss in. 40, 70, 100 grand a year, it's all made up. Ain't no one I've ever met earns more than £30k.

Tristan   Has anyone you've ever met got a first in a pure maths degree?

Jen   Well . . . no . . . but –

Tristan   But what?

Jen   But it's easy for you to say when you're sat there and I'm sat here, cos right now all it is to me is a fuck tonne of cash and a handful of maybes. You've actually no idea how hard it is.

Tristan   You know what, you're right. It's hard. Really fucking hard. There's gonna be people here who've had tutors all the way through school, the work gets ten times more complex and the professors won't all take easily to your straight-up style.

Jen   What are you trying to say?

Tristan   That if you think you've got it hard now, well, you come to uni and you're going to have to graft way more than you ever have before if you want to be top of your class. You'll have to apply yourself, and people's opinions of you matter so you can't just walk out because you don't like the tutor and still expect to get a first. You know what, you're right, you're probably not cut out for it.

Jen   What?

Tristan   That's what you want me to say, isn't it? Go back home, look after your mum and stack your shelves. I bet you're damn good at it.

Jen   Are you being sarky?

Tristan   Not at all. But you don't want this clearly, so why waste your time?

He allows her time to answer but she's got nothing. He knows he's got her stumped.

You ever played the lottery, Jen?

Jen   On my sixteenth birthday. And I get a scratch card at Christmas.

Tristan   So you're willing to back some crazy odds then? What are the odds of a girl from Bradford backing herself instead: grafting, becoming really successful, and taking home a really juicy pay packet?

Jen   Slim I'd say.

Tristan   Not as slim as the lottery. You gonna play the odds, Jen?

Pause. She's humbled.

Jen   Maybe.

Tristan   There's a small scholarship available which I can point you in the direction of and I can get you a list of random rich people that you can write letters to who might support you. Crazy, I know, I thought that too.

Jen   You're wrong in the head, you.

Tristan   For giving a shit?

Jen   Yeh. A bit.

Tristan   It's up to you.

Jen   Thanks.

(*She means it.*) I don't have to hug you do I?

   Tristan *is amused*.

Scene Eleven: The Street

   Late September, a Sunday afternoon. **Jen** *is leaving her house to
   go back to uni and sees* **Stacey** *stood outside.*

Stacey   Hey, stranger.

Jen   Hey.

   A silence.

Jen   Y'alright?

Stacey   Fair to middling. You?

Jen   Fine.

Stacey   I tried calling.

Jen   Been busy.

Stacey   Can we talk?

Jen   I've got plans. Sorry.

Stacey   Plans?

Jen   Back in Newcastle. There's a mixer thing.

Stacey   Eh?

Jen   Basically a few pre-drinks.

Stacey   You going out?

Jen   Yeh, I'd invite you but it's obviously . . .

Stacey   It's fine.

Jen   What you doing down here anyway?

Stacey   I needed to talk to you.

Jen   Why?

Stacey   Just wanted to.

Jen   Right. It's not great timing. You could've called.

Stacey   You wouldn't have answered.

Jen   I might've.

She wouldn't have.

Stacey   They like you up there then?

Jen   They're nice actually yeh.

Stacey   Just seems a bit rich that's all.

Jen   What you mean?

Stacey   You know what I mean.

Jen   I actually like them.

Stacey   You might, but you're hardly similar.

Jen   Why are you here?

Stacey   I wanted –

Jen   Don't give me some bullshit about wanting to reach out, make amends or some bollocks. Just come out with it.

A pause.

Stacey   Can I stay at yours?

Jen   What?

Stacey   Just for tonight and maybe a couple of days?

Jen   I'm not here though am I? I thought you were shacked up with him now.

Stacey   I am but . . .

Jen   Fuck's sake, will you just come out with it?

Stacey We argued. Bad this time. We were play fighting and then he accidentally hurt himself – kicked the bedpost and then this look. In his eye. Just this look. And I should've said sorry but I didn't. I just ran.

Jen *is proud, but doesn't show it.*

Stacey I just need somewhere to stay – for a couple of days.

Jen What about your mam's?

Stacey I can't. He'll find me. I'm scared for the twins.

Jen So you want to bring him to my mum's? When she's on her own? Are you off your head? I'm gonna miss the train.

Stacey They've been your mates for like 10 seconds.

Jen I've got class tomorrow.

Stacey They'll understand.

Jen I need to give a good impression.

Stacey Since when did you care?

Jen Since I have to.

Stacey I just thought that –

Jen That you could come crawling back to me until you've sorted your little spat with Nathan and can fuck off back to him again – well sorry, but I've actually got somewhere to be.

Stacey It's not like that Jen, I swear.

Jen I'm gonna be late. I can't miss this train. I can't afford another ticket.

Stacey I wouldn't come if I didn't really need to.

Jen Typical Stacey!

Stacey That's not – just a couple of nights, please. I'll stay on the couch.

Jen   Mum's just about holding herself together, she can't carry you as well.

Stacey   She won't even notice I'm there.

Jen   No. It's too much. I have to stick to my plan.

Stacey   You don't plan, Jen.

Jen   I do. Because it turns out when you don't, you get left on the street with a fiver at your feet.

Stacey   What the bollocks are you on about?

Jen   That night. Shit, my train. Bye.

  Jen *goes to leave.* **Stacey** *calls after her.*

Stacey   The Jen I know wouldn't walk out on her mate. She wouldn't walk out on anyone. She might look like her dad but she isn't one single bit like him.

Jen   Don't try manipulate me Stace – it won't work. I'm sorry, I can't help you. I want to, I do. But literally, I gotta be at the station in 20 minutes, I'm getting the bus, I'm already cutting it fine.

Stacey   I have nowhere to go. You'll make me go back to him.

Jen   I don't make you do anything.

Stacey   You make me do everything.

Jen   How is this my fault?

Stacey   You're sending me back to him, knowing full well.

Jen   You chose him. You chose him over me. What did you want me to do? Sit here waiting for you to come back to me?

Stacey   You're fine on your own, you always say that. Jen doesn't need anyone. Except to be liked by some backstabbing basic bitches.

Jen   You don't know anything about them. They're good people, nice people. Rich, but nice.

Stacey   You've changed your tune.

Jen   Maybe I have.

Stacey   Good, but you listen here, I'm not gonna be at your beck and call trying to second guess what this 'new you' wants from me. I'm tired, Jen, and I've got a lot of figuring out to do. My life's a shit storm but I'm not going to stand here and beg you for help. You're either there or you're not.

Jen   I would've been there all summer, whatever you needed, just like we said. But you didn't want anything. Summer's been and gone now. You can't just wipe away what you did because you suddenly need me.

> **Jen** *starts to walk off.* **Stacey** *is shocked; this person isn't* **Jen**. *She screams after her.*

Stacey   Jen, don't –

> **Stacey** *is left alone. When did* **Jen** *get like this? She is crushed. She exits, nervous as hell.*

Scene Twelve: Look What the Cat Dragged In

Two weeks later. A weekend. **Leanne**'s *kitchen. Evening.* **Leanne** *is in her rather unattractive nightshirt. She is looking at a Crunchie bar in her hand eyeing it up. She has some spilt crumbs and melted chocolate down herself from an earlier snack.*

There is a knock at the door.

Leanne   Who the bleeding hell's this at this time? Oh fuck off will ya, me and this Crunchie are having some one-on-one time.

> *She heaves herself up and goes to the door.*

I'm sure this bleeding menopause has spread to my fucking joints now. Bastards.

She answers the door. **Stacey** *is stood there, her hair is wet, and her make-up has run down her face. It may have been raining.*

Leanne   You look like shit.

Stacey   Thanks.

Leanne   Jen's not here.

Stacey   I thought she was back this weekend.

Leanne   She's at the Chatha's. Come in, pet.

Leanne *invites* **Stacey** *in.*

Leanne   Brew?

Stacey   Please.

Leanne *puts the kettle on and talks as she does.*

Leanne   You're not sharing me Crunchie though. I need that chuffing Friday feeling after the day I've had. Between Alison two doors down and the bloody audit at work I've just about had it. I'm bordering on prescribing myself everything under the sun and seeing myself off just for the hell of it.

Leanne *laughs then throws* **Stacey** *a packet of make-up wipes.*

Leanne   Take it off then. Your make-up.

Stacey *takes a wipe and starts removing her make-up.* **Leanne** *gives her some space to see if she wants to speak.* **Stacey** *doesn't want to speak.* **Leanne** *busies herself making the teas.*

Leanne   Our Jen's doing well at uni. Really took a shine to her they have. She's took some shifts up at Tesco Extra too. Stacking and that. Says she finds it therapeutic. She'd be mortified if she knew I was telling you. But I'm just so bleeding proud of her. She just cracks on does our Jen, and when she knows what she wants to do, she's right on with it.

Leanne *gives* **Stacey** *the tea.*

Stacey   Thanks.

Once again, **Leanne** *leaves space for* **Stacey** *to speak but she doesn't.* **Leanne** *doesn't know exactly what has happened but she can put two and two together and make four. She is aware of the* **Nathan** *situation but just won't push* **Stacey** *to say anything she isn't ready to say.*

Leanne   Hey, did our Jen tell you that Dean's taking me to London next month? The chap from the boxing. Well, he's running a self-defence course down there, a weekend one. So they've put him up and I'm going with him. I've never been to London. I'm made up. A whole weekend, just me and him. And I know he's not really your age or anything but he is properly fit. In both senses of the word, like fit, because of the boxing and that but also like *phwoar* fit.

Stacey *smiles slightly.*

Leanne   You've got a beautiful little smile you have. You're a very beautiful girl.

The smile instantly disappears. **Stacey** *isn't comfortable in herself and doesn't believe that she could ever be beautiful.*

Leanne   Our Jen misses you heaps you know. She'd kill me for saying it, but I can just tell. She misses having you around all the time. You two are like, I don't know, Bill and Ben, or Ant and Dec, or the chuffing Chuckle Brothers when you get together. I miss having you around as well. Hearing you two giggling away about goodness knows what upstairs warms my stone cold heart. It's special that.

Leanne *sits next to* **Stacey** *and allows another moment.* **Stacey** *looks up for a second but then back to her brew.*

Leanne   This bleeding menopause is getting worse. The forgetfulness, it's like I have these complete blanks and I've no idea what the bleeding hell just happened. The other day I'd forgotten to take my HRT, that was the first thing, and then I was at work and I couldn't remember Dr Karhan's bleeding name for the life of me, so I just had to point and tell the poor biddy to go in the door on the left. Then Dean comes to pick me up at 7 and I'd no idea where we were meant to be going, but we'd made the arrangements just the night before. Somedays I think I've gone completely off my tree. Absolute la-la land. And don't start me on the emotions, I started crying the other day in Tesco cause this young lad reached a can of them sugar-free beans down for me from the top shelf. I cried at him. He nodded and shuffled away, and I just stood there and cried for a further five minutes because I thought it was so sweet that he did it and I didn't even ask. Oh, it's fun and games isn't it.

> **Stacey** *smiles at* **Leanne**.

Stacey   Thanks for this. Really.

Leanne   It's only a brew, pet. I saw your mam in the med centre last week.

Stacey   Milo?

Leanne   The other one this time. The runs. Said she didn't think you'd stayed in your own bed for about three weeks . . .

Stacey   How would she know, she's still on nights.

Leanne   A mother knows, we can just sense it. I don't know if I dobbed you in, because I didn't know if I was meant to lie and say that you'd moved in with us but I just sort of nodded and styled it out I think. Sorry.

Stacey   It's alright. I've not lied, I've just not kept her in the loop really.

Leanne   You're always welcome here, you know that, no matter what's going on with you and Jen, you can come here and drink me tea anytime.

> **Stacey** *smiles and then realises that she hates herself even more because people are nice to her. She crumbles.*

Stacey   I don't know what I did to deserve everyone being so nice to me.

Leanne *jumps in and wraps her arms around her. The positioning is awkward but it doesn't matter.*

Leanne   Now, now, now. Let's have none of that. You are very dearly loved, you know that. By all of us. Jen included, even if she can be a stubborn little swine at times. We're not good to you out of charity, pet. We look out for you because we love you, because you're wonderful and clever, and pretty and you've got such a beauty little heart. Honest.

*Stacey is done in, she can't hold the barriers up anymore, she is vulnerable. **Leanne** cradles her and snuggles her.*

*Leanne kisses her forehead, **Stacey** for a second is unsure how she feels about being kissed on the forehead, but it is just **Leanne**, it is fine, it is safe. **Stacey** eventually wipes her eyes and composes herself.*

Stacey   Thanks. For everything. I – I should be getting off.

Leanne   Are you sure?

Stacey   I need to go.

Leanne   Have you got somewhere to go to?

Stacey   Might try out my own bed, see if it's missed me. Make sure it's not been turned into a playroom or something.

Leanne   That sounds like a great idea.

Stacey   Thanks. Again. Sorry.

Leanne   Alright, stop saying thanks, it's getting too much now.

Stacey   Don't tell Jen, please.

Leanne   I won't, but you should. She'd love to hear from you. Properly.

Stacey   I will. In time.

Leanne   Alright, here, do you want this Crunchie?

Stacey   I couldn't.

Leanne   Please. I shouldn't be having it anyway. Dean's got me into training and I'm on a meal plan thing. Moment of weakness. Blame the menopause. I think you need that Friday feeling a bit more than I do anyway.

Stacey   Thanks. You're too good –

Leanne   Oi, zip it, I'll have none of this too good nonsense. You're worth every last honeycomb crumb of that bleeding chocolate bar. I'll go back to googling images of ice cream with salted caramel sauce.

Stacey   Thanks.

Leanne   Do you want me to book you a taxi? It's getting pretty late.

Stacey   I'll walk it, I need the fresh air.

Leanne   I'm not sure . . .

Stacey   I'll be fine. I probably look more of a threat right now with the state of me.

Leanne   You're beautiful. Text me when you're home safe.

Stacey   Will do.

Leanne   Promise?

Stacey   Promise. Thanks again Leanne.

Leanne   Don't even mention it. Now you get on your way before it gets too dark and I worry myself silly.

Stacey   Love you, Leanne.

Leanne   Love you too, pet. Off you trot.

> **Stacey** *smiles, braces herself and leaves.* **Leanne** *shuts the door, gets a satsuma and peels it as she watches* **Stacey** *out the window. She receives a text from Dean and looks at her phone.*

Scene Thirteen: Oh Shit!

The street outside **Leanne**'*s house. Immediately after.* **Stacey** *is walking home. A van rolls up outside.* **Nathan** *gets out and speaks to* **Stacey**.

The following conversation is heated but voices aren't to be raised. The street doesn't hear anything.

Nathan   Where've you been, I've been worried sick?

Stacey   None of your business.

Nathan   Have you been with Jen?

Stacey   No.

Nathan   Liar.

Stacey   Leave me alone.

Nathan   Come home, love.

Stacey   I'm going home.

Nathan   I'm sorry, love. I shouldn't have called it off. I didn't mean what I said. I didn't think you'd just up and leave like that.

Stacey   What did you expect me to do?

Nathan   I don't know . . . but you can't be wandering the streets at this time like some slapper.

Stacey   It's none of your business what I do anymore. You don't want me remember? What was it you said, 'I've let my standards slip'?

Nathan   You're twisting my words again, don't –

Stacey   I'm not, Nathan, that's what you said, clear as day. I've let my standards slip. I've given my everything for you, my whole fucking everything but it's not good enough is it? It will never be good enough. I've given up Newcastle, Jen, Seabrook crisps, I don't even wear lipgloss anymore. I keep trying to be good enough Nathan but I still can't get it right. I don't know what you want from me.

Nathan   I just want you to be the best version of yourself is all.

Stacey   What if this is the best version of myself?

Nathan   Come on, Stace, you look like –

Stacey   Don't say another fucking word. I'm going home.

   Stacey *starts to walk off.*

Nathan   Stacey, stop.

Stacey   Leave me alone, Nathan.

Nathan   Stace!

   Nathan *grabs* **Stacey***; he is gripping tight and getting angry.*

Stacey (*calmly*)   Get your hands off me. We're over, Nathan. That's what you said. Now just let me go home.

Nathan   You're coming with me. It's not over. We can work through this. Come on!

   He starts to pull her towards his van.

Stacey   GET YOUR FUCKING HANDS OFF ME!

   Nathan *is taken aback by her reaction but doesn't let go.* **Stacey** *starts to struggle.*

Stacey   You're hurting!

   Leanne *overhears, looks out the window. Jumps to her feet and rushes outside.*

Nathan   You're making this look bad. Stacey, just get in, we can talk when we get home, I've put the heated seats –

Leanne   Oi. You! Let her go, now!

Nathan   Who are you?

   Nathan *loosens his grip on* **Stacey** *but keeps her close.*

Leanne I said, let her go!

Stacey Leanne!

Nathan It's not what it looks like, she's just –

Leanne I don't care what it looks like, you're going to let her go right now or I chop your bleeding balls off, understand?

    Nathan *lets go of* **Stacey**. **Stacey** *rushes to* **Leanne**.

Leanne Now get your scratty little arse off my street.

Nathan (*to* **Stacey**)   Stace – I just want to talk. Listen, love, you don't need to let anyone get involved in our business.

Leanne Oi, you'll not say another word to her.

(*To* **Stacey**.) Go inside pet, call Jen.

    Nathan *sees red*.

Nathan Jen? Call Jen? Are you fucking joking? The last thing she needs is to speak to that slag.

    Leanne *sees red*.

Leanne Don't you fucking dare!

Nathan That bitch is everything that's wrong with our relationship. If it weren't for her –

Leanne You bad mouth my girl again and I'm warning you.

Nathan Don't fucking threaten me, what you gonna do, coffin dodger?

Leanne I'm fifty fucking one. And you better watch yourself cos my boyfriend's a black belt.

Nathan He isn't fucking here though is he? Your little tramp of a daughter has ruined my fucking life.

Leanne Call her a tramp one more time.

Nathan   Everyone knows that she's filth. She gave half the lads on this estate the fucking clap. Come on, Stace – enough is enough.

> **Nathan** *grabs* **Stacey***'s arm and tries to drag her to the van like a rag doll.* **Leanne** *follows and tries to pull* **Stacey** *back.* **Nathan** *turns and hits* **Leanne***. An intake of breath. Even* **Nathan** *can't believe what he's done.* **Leanne** *has now lost it.*

> **Jen** *enters just as* **Leanne** *does a spectacular self-defence judo move on* **Nathan** *and* **Stacey** *steps back.* **Nathan** *hits the deck.*

> **Leanne** *picks him up and drags him to his van. She opens the door and throws him in it.*

Leanne   Now fuck off!

Jen   Mum!

> **Nathan** *looks a little bit stunned by the whole thing.* **Leanne** *goes to* **Stacey***, who is just stood there, also in awe.* **Leanne** *turns to audience.*

> **Jen** *rushes to* **Leanne***.*

Leanne   And you can fuck off too, Alison, you nosey bitch. Mind your own fucking business.

> **Leanne** *takes* **Stacey** *nearer the house.* **Stacey** *is a little shaken but she's ok. She smiles at* **Leanne***.* **Jen** *is worried about* **Leanne***.*

Stacey   I . . .

Leanne (*still reeling*)   Squirming little fucking rat! Not much of a man that one is he?

Jen   Mum, what the fuck was that?

Leanne   I think you two need to talk.

Jen   We're not really talking.

Leanne   Are you having me on? I've just practically earned an Olympic gold in my self-defence and you can't even – Oh you girls! You need your heads banging together, you do.

Stacey   I'm sorry, Leanne, and thanks for – it's just – I want to go home, I hope you don't mind – I just – I want to see my mum.

Leanne   I'll book you a taxi, but you two have to sort this out!

> **Leanne** *exits. Both girls are taken aback and quietly sit down. They stare at each other silently.*

Jen   She can't cope with this right now.

Stacey   I know.

Jen   I . . .

> *There is nothing now. She gets up to leave and calls into the house.*

Stacey   Thanks, Leanne.

> *She leaves.* **Jen** *is alone. When did it get to this?*

> *Fade to black.*

Scene Fourteen: In the Queue

> *A week later. The first Thursday in October.* **Jen** *and* **Stacey** *are stood in the queue for Club Ocean. 'Mr Brightside/Sex on Fire' can be heard playing inside. It's awkward.*

Jen   When's your other mates getting here then?

Stacey   Dunno. They said they'd drop me a text when they set off.

Jen   They texted you?

Stacey   Nah. Not yet.

Jen   Cool.

Silence.

How's Nathan?

Stacey   Dunno. Don't know where he's at to be honest.

Jen   You talking?

Stacey   Nah. Not really.

Jen   Cool.

Silence.

You doing well at college then?

Stacey   Dunno. It's more writing than dancing at the minute.

Jen   You quitting?

Stacey   Nah. Not right now.

Jen   Good.

Silence.

Stacey   How's Newcastle?

Jen   Not bad.

Stacey   You enjoy it?

Jen   Sometimes.

Silence.

Jen   I'm busting for a piss.

Stacey   Me too.

Jen   It's taking forever.

Silence.

Stacey   I like that top.

Jen   Well, you can't have it.

Stacey   Primark's finest?

Jen   New Look sale. £5.

Stacey   Bargain.

Silence.

Jen   Rack looks good.

Stacey   Doubled up.

Jen   What?

Stacey   Chicken fillets. I doubled up.

*Jen smiles at **Stacey**. **Stacey** smiles back.*

Jen   Let's see then.

*Stacey lets **Jen** look in her bra.*

Jen   You've done a proper good job there. Just move that one . . .

*Jen slightly readjusts one of the chicken fillets for **Stacey**. We hear a voice from off.*

Male Voice (*from off*)   Whhheyyyy. Lick her tits, you filthy lezza.

Jen/Stacey   FUCK OFF!

They turn back and look at each other for a moment. They burst out laughing. They stop laughing.

Stacey   I missed you.

Jen   I think I jumped the gun you know.

Stacey   With what?

Jen   The whole uni thing.

Stacey   What?

Jen   It's really fucking hard you know.

Stacey   Mate, you're basically Einstein with great tits.

Jen   It's not the maths bit. That's just imaginary numbers and other bollocks – same shit different day. It's the other stuff. £1.50 a meal! I've had toasted potato cakes for a week straight cos they were 15p in the Whoopsie clearance aisle. And £28 for everything else? These guys go Starbucks every day – mate, that's £17.50 for one coffee and that's just on school days. I can't keep up with 'em.

Stacey   It's only three years, get your head down, you'll out-maths them all and you'll get a big posh job. Your mam'll go down to four days a week.

Jen   Yeh. I know. I just feel like – I'm up to my tits in debt and I've got to choose between sambuca and fucking graph paper. It's squared paper with smaller fucking squares, why's it cost so fucking much? Is this what I want for the rest of my life? I didn't have to choose when it was just me and you, but now you've got all this, I worry. I worry that I picked wrong.

Stacey   What is it that you think I have, Jen?

Jen   College and mates and you just know that you're on the right path.

Stacey   A college course where not even the teachers want to be there. A group of people who I'm terrified of getting close to in case they hurt me like he did. I'm a shell, Jen. Empty. I don't even know the person that drags her arse to that damn studio everyday.

Jen   Bit dark, mate.

Stacey   True though.

Jen   He really fucked you up didn't he?

Stacey   Just a bit.

Jen   You'll survive, mate, you always do.

Stacey   Tried to shag a guy last week, Johnny Parks, from the drama course, we'd been texting. Got halfway through, started freaking out, hopped off and cried for about thirty minutes straight. Then he offered me a fromage frais. I ate it and left. Now he's spreading round that I'm a psycho.

Stacey *is embarrassed.* **Jen** *tries not to laugh but then can't contain it.*

Jen   A fromage fucking frais.

Stacey   Yeh. Strawberry and apricot. His sister's apparently.

Jen   Mam told me she's been checking up on you.

Stacey   Didn't know if she would.

Jen   Can't keep her trap shut that one.

Stacey   She's been really good wi' me, you know.

Jen *smiles.*

Jen   I didn't know whether to call or what.

Stacey   Would've been nice.

Jen   I know. I'm sorry. I should've – I could've – I didn't know what to do.

Stacey   It's not your fault.

Jen   I know. But I could've been better. And I know I'm up there but I could've been –

Stacey   You're here now aren't you?

Jen   Yeh.

Stacey   I didn't know if you were going to come.

Jen   Don't be daft.

Stacey   I dunno, I just thought with everything, that you might –

Jen   What?

Stacey   Be, sort of, done.

Jen   Oh fuck off, you melt. I'm more than that and you know it.

Stacey   Yeh.

Jen   Besides, I wouldn't miss Adam from *Geordie Shore*. His forearms are the best thing since sliced bread. And obviously we said that we'd . . .

Stacey   Yeh.

A pause.

Jen   This lass on my course, she's a singer, doing a music video. I told her about your choreography, she said she'd be up for meeting you. It's not paid but you can stay with me, if that's what you want.

Stacey   I actually did a music video, last week. Got £50 for it. It's no David Guetta but it's actually not bad.

Jen   How many dancers?

Stacey   Just me.

Jen   You actually in it?

Stacey   The dancer they booked dropped out last minute, so I stepped up.

Jen   Fuck me, that's ballsy for you, Stacey Blackwell.

Stacey   Can't hide in the shadows anymore, can I?

Jen   Remember when you played Munchkin 8 in *The Wizard of Oz*, year 9, and you tore up the stage.

Stacey   I did the worm.

Jen   You were brilliant, mate. Like fucking fantastic. Like I'd never seen someone so good. The way you just seemed . . . free. You just had it, whatever it is. That something extra. Totally upstaged the boring ass Dorothy.

Stacey   That was Sarah-Jane Jacobs wasn't it?

Jen   Fuuuuck!

It's still a bit awkward.

Bloody hell, I'm proper busting for a piss.

Stacey   You got any tissues?

Jen   Think so.

She rummages in bag.

Not got tissues, but got some napkins from Nando's, that'll do the trick.

She rummages in her bag still. She starts passing things to **Stacey**. *She passes her a bottle of water.*

Stacey   Oooh, Voddy.

She opens the bottle.

Jen   Nah, just water. Geordie Voddy is well pricey. Hold this a sec.

She passes a purse, a lipgloss, a pair of sunglasses, a whistle. A condom in packet. **Stacey** *grabs the condom.*

Stacey   Bloody hell! Who's this and what've you done with my Jen?!

Jen   FUCK!

Stacey   What?

Jen   I think I forgot my ID.

Stacey   Don't be daft. You always have it. It'll be in there somewhere.

Jen   It's not.

Stacey   Isn't it in your purse?

Jen   No, I took it out to fill in some form for uni and left it on the kitchen table.

Stacey   Have you checked all the pockets?

Jen Yeh. It's definitely on the kitchen table. I remember telling myself. I can't believe I –

Stacey Let me look.

>   **Stacey** *takes the bag and rummages through.*

Jen I'm telling you it's not there.

>   **Stacey** *finishes looking in the bag.*

Stacey Yeh, it's not there.

Jen FUCK!

Stacey It'll be alright, the bouncers know us.

Jen They've got stricter, literally no ID, no entry, 'cause they had a thing with that fourteen-year-old lass.

Stacey I'm pretty sure if we ask them.

Jen They won't let us in.

Stacey I'm going to go ask 'em.

>   **Stacey** *walks off.* **Jen** *rummages in her bag again before giving up.* **Stacey** *returns.*

Jen So?

Stacey They won't let us in.

Jen What did I say?

Stacey Worth a try.

Jen Look, babe, you've had a rough time, you go in, your mates will be on their way soon anyways.

Stacey I ain't going in without you.

Jen Don't be a doillum. I'll be alright, I'll just get a cab. I'd invite you back but Mam's got that boxing guy staying over so it's mega awkward.

Stacey That's going well then.

Jen   Too well. Put it this way, there's nothing discreet about a six foot three man and my mam's ancient mattress. Look, you need to let your hair down, you need this. Go in, have a blast, the usual suspects will be in there, Party Paul, you can hang with them until your mates get here.

Stacey   I don't want to.

Jen   Sorry, babe, I'm fucking raging at myself but there's nowt I can do.

Jen starts zipping her bag up. A beat.

Stacey   Wanna share twenty nuggets and stay in Maccies till 3 a.m.?

Jen   Stace –

Stacey   It's past 12 anyway, so it's three quid entry. Screw Ocean, let's get a sharebox.

Jen   What about your mates?

Stacey   Fuck 'em. If they wanted to be here, they'd be here wouldn't they?

Jen   You sure?

Stacey   Walking round Bradford city centre, desperate for a piss, in the freezing cold – never been more sure! Come on.

They start walking off linking arms. They look to the wall where they pissed earlier. It's a bad idea.

Jen   It can wait till Maccies.

They laugh and exit.

Printed in the USA
CPSIA information can be obtained
at www.ICGtesting.com
LVHW020856171024
794056LV00002B/559